Italian Renaissance

Martin Roberts

Longman Group UK Limited Longman House,
Burnt Mill, Harlow, Essex, CM20 2JE, England
and Associated Companies throughout the World.

© Longman Group UK Limited 1992

First published 1992
ISBN 0 582 08252 8

Set in 11/15pt Bodoni (Lasercomp)
Printed and bound by
BPCC Hazell Books, Aylesbury, Bucks, England

It is the publisher's policy to use paper
manufactured from sustainable forests.

Designed by: Roger Walton Studio
Illustrated by: Nadine Wickenden (maps)
            Mitch Stuart (page 20)
            Kathy Baxendale (pages 13, 39)
Cover photograph: Detail from Procession of the
Magi, Medici Palace Chapel. Bridgeman.

We are grateful to the following for permission to
reproduce photographs:

Ancient Art & Architecture Collection, pages 26
above, 27 above, 61 above, 83 above; Osvaldo
Böhm, page 35; The Bridgeman Art Library,
pages 11 below, 21 below, Carmine Church,
Florence, 27 centre, 44 below, Galleria Degli
Uffizi, Florence, 47 below, Victoria and Albert
Museum, London, 52, Galleria Degli Uffizi,
Florence, 56, 59 below, From Quaderini di
Anatomia vol 2; Folio 3v, 60, Louvre, Paris, 71
right, 82 above Louvre, Paris; The British
Museum, page 71 left; E. T. Archive, page 59
above; Michael Holford, pages 61 below, 73, 82
below, 83 below, 85 right; Kunsthistorisches
Museum, Vienna, page 67; Mansell Collection,
page 81; The National Gallery, London, page 23,
37 below left, 37 below right; National Museum,
Cracow, page 40 above (Lukasz Schuster);
Paternoster Associates, page 85 left; Royal
Library, Windsor Castle. Reproduced by gracious
permission of Her Majesty Queen Elizabeth II,
page 40 below; SCALA, pages 4, 5, 6, 10, 11
above, 14, 15, 19, 20, 21 above, The Baptistry,
Museo Dell'Opera, Florence, 22, The Baptistry,
Museo Dell'Opera, Florence, 24, 26 centre, 26
below, 27 below, Santa Maria Novella, Florence,
28, Santa Maria Novella, Florence, 29, Piazza Del
Santo, Padua, 32, Vatican Gallery della Carte
Geografiche, 37 above, Museo Civico, Turino, 38,
Accademia, Venice, 41, 44 above, Pinacoteca,

Vatican, 45, Stanze di Rafaello, Vatican, 46, 47
above, S. Pietro in Montorio, Rome, 51, Santa
Maria Novella, Florence, 53, Museo di San Marco,
Florence, 55, 57, Louvre, Paris, 62, 68, Palace
Vecchio, Florence, 70, 72, Great Hall, Palazzo
della Cancelleria, Rome, 75, Palace Vecchio,
Florence, 87, Ducal Palace, Urbino; Thomas-
Photos, Oxford, page 78.

We are unable to trace the copyright holder of the
following on pages 12, 30, 48 and would
appreciate receiving any information that would
enable us to do so.

Contents

Introduction

1 **The Piazza della Signoria in Florence.**

Few cities are more popular with holiday-makers than the Italian cities of Florence, Venice and Rome. Tourists come from all over the world in such large numbers that the citizens of Florence and Venice sometimes wonder how they can cope with many more.

Why do people come in their millions to visit these places? It is partly because they are old and interesting, and partly because they are the homes of some of the finest paintings, statues and buildings ever made. Many of these works of art date from a short period, from 1400 to 1530, which is now known as the Italian Renaissance.

French and German historians first used the word 'renaissance', which means rebirth or revival, about the Italian artistic achievements of 1400–1530 because the Italian artists and writers of those years believed that they were leading to a rebirth or revival of classical civilisation. We use the term 'classical civilisation' to mean the civilisation of ancient Greece and Rome, which had been at its best between 500 BC and AD150.

In the opinion of the Italians of the Renaissance period, classical civilisation had been the high point of human history. They believed people

2 **The Piazza San Marco in Venice.**

then had been ruled well, had lived in fine cities or fertile countryside and were usually happy and prosperous. In this classical civilisation, brilliant writers and excellent artists had flourished. In contrast, or so the Renaissance Italians thought, the thousand or so years since the decline of the ancient Roman Empire and their own time, the so-called Middle Ages, were a barbaric and uncivilised time. They agreed with the poet Petrarch (1304–74) that 'the world was about to break out of the darkness . . . and return to the pure brightness of ancient Greece and Rome'.

Yet, while Renaissance Italy had this great respect for and borrowed many ideas and artistic styles from ancient Greece and Rome, its writers and artists had ideas and styles of their own. Indeed, many people today prefer the art of the Italian Renaissance to the art of the classical period. Italian Renaissance ideas and styles spread quickly to other European countries and brought important changes to European ways of thinking.

This book describes this key moment in European civilisation and explains its main causes, its achievements and the changes which it brought, first to Italy and then to Europe.

3 The Piazza San Pietro in the Vatican, Rome.

1 Florence in the fifteenth century

The Renaissance began in Florence, the most important city in the region of northern Italy known as Tuscany.

Look at source 1.

1 What are the largest buildings in this city?

2 In what main ways does it differ from where you live?

3 a) If people wanted to use the picture as a record of what Florence was really like, how accurate do you think it would be?

b) How might historians test its accuracy?

4 List three important things about city life which this source does not show. What different sources would you use to find out about these things?

Why was Florence an important city?

Trade and Commerce

Florence stood at the meeting point of important trade-routes at a time when northern Italy was the centre of European trade. With Venice and Milan (see sources 2 and 3) it was a leading centre of industry and commerce (buying and selling goods). Compared to the sprawling cities of modern Europe with their millions of inhabitants, fifteenth-century Florence, with a population of about

1 Florence drawn in 1480.

KEY

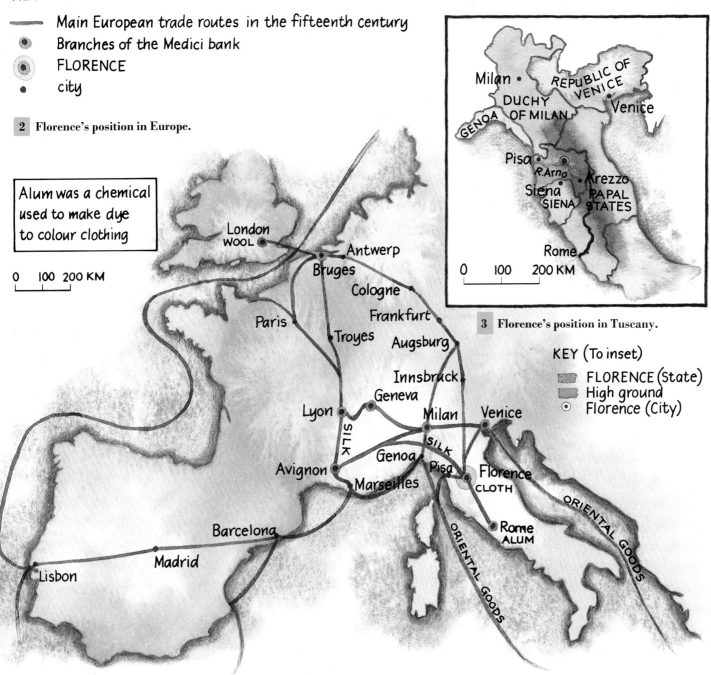

─── Main European trade routes in the fifteenth century
◉ Branches of the Medici bank
◉ FLORENCE
• city

2 Florence's position in Europe.

Alum was a chemical used to make dye to colour clothing

0 100 200 KM

London
WOOL

Antwerp

Bruges

Cologne

Paris

Frankfurt

Troyes

Augsburg

Innsbruck

Geneva

Lyon

SILK

Milan

Venice

Avignon

Genoa

SILK

Pisa

Florence
CLOTH

Marseilles

Barcelona

Madrid

Rome
ALUM

Lisbon

ORIENTAL GOODS

ORIENTAL GOODS

3 Florence's position in Tuscany.

Milan •

REPUBLIC OF VENICE

DUCHY OF MILAN

Venice

GENOA

Pisa •

R. Arno

Arezzo

Siena •

SIENA

PAPAL STATES

Rome •

0 100 200 KM

KEY (To inset)

▨ FLORENCE (State)
▨ High ground
◉ Florence (City)

---

5 What were the main trade-routes linking Florence with other parts of Europe?

6 Give four reasons why the geographical situation of Florence helped it to become a great city.

7 Explain the link between English wool, Roman alum and the rich cloth industry of Florence.

8 a) List the cities outside Florence in which the Medici banking family had branches.

b) Why do you think the Medici chose these cities?

c) Why were they also keen to get control of alum supplies?

70,000 in 1400, seems small. But it was large for those days. London, England's largest city, only had about 35,000 people. In fact, Florence was one of Europe's largest cities and among the wealthiest. It was famous for its cloth and silk, its dyeing, its jewellery and its metalwork. The houses you can see in source 1 are mostly the homes of merchants and workpeople, and usually included their shops and workrooms.

Its richest citizens were its bankers, of whom there were more than seventy in 1422. They owed much to the earlier bankers of the city who, in 1252, had issued a small gold coin called the florin. Unlike many other coin producers of the time, they kept the gold of the florin pure. Traders all over Italy and in many other countries were happy to use it because of its reputation for purity. By 1400, there were about 2 million florins in circulation and some Florentine bankers, like the Medici, had branches in other European countries (see source 3).

Florence becomes more powerful

Florence was one of a number of independent states in Italy, each of which was keen to increase its power at the expense of its neighbours. The largest states were Milan and Venice in the north; the Papal States ruled by the Pope from

4 The main states of Italy in the early fifteenth century.

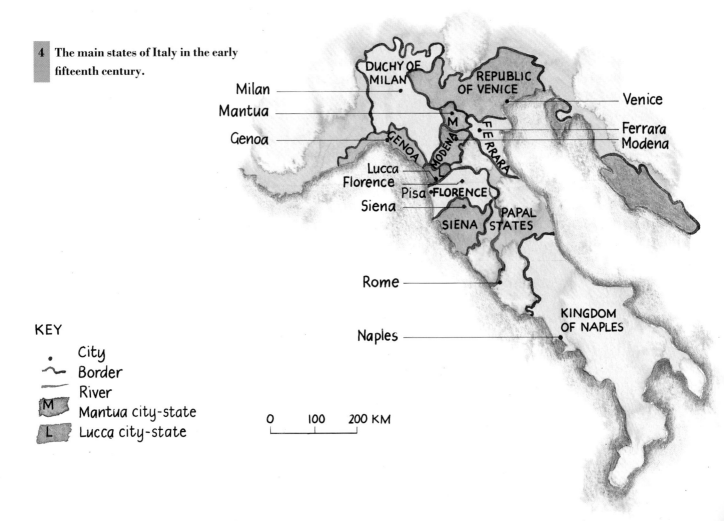

KEY

- • City
- 〜 Border
- — River
- M Mantua city-state
- L Lucca city-state

0   100   200 KM

Rome in the centre, and the Kingdom of Naples in the south. Those which had grown up round one important city, like Florence, Venice and Milan, were known as city-states.

The Florentines were not good soldiers and they preferred to pay others to fight for them. In the early fifteenth century they did well; partly by luck, partly by money and partly by choosing the right friends at the right time. In 1402, Giangaleazzo Visconti, the ambitious ruler of Milan, who was their deadliest enemy, suddenly died just as he was about to add Florence to his possessions. Much the same happened in 1414 when Ladislao, King of Naples, advanced dangerously towards the city, only to die of illness in the nick of time.

The Florentine government usually tried to stay friends with the Venetians since Milan was also their enemy. In 1406, Florence won the important port of Pisa, in 1413 Arezzo and 1421 Livorno. By 1454 it controlled the whole Arno valley.

The Florentine Republic

Most European states had rulers like kings, dukes or counts who were hereditary; that is, they ruled because their father or some other relative had ruled before them. Milan, for example, was ruled by dukes from the Visconti family, and England and France had kings or queens.

Florence, however, was a republic, which meant that its rulers were elected. The 37-strong ruling council, called the Signoria, was elected every two months and in times of crisis special larger committees, called *balie*, were also elected. So Florence was used to frequent elections. Also, since 3,000 government posts each year went to citizens chosen by lot, in a kind of draw, rather than by election, an unusually large number of people were actively involved in politics.

The Florentines patted themselves on the back and believed that their free and lively republic was much better than other forms of personal rule where rulers decided everything with little thought for the wishes of their subjects. Yet, in fact, most adults in Florence had no political power worth speaking of. Women could not vote, nor could most working men. Only the merchants and better-off craftsmen had the vote and could hold an office in the government.

Real power in Florence rested in the hands of the male members of a small number of rich families like the Alberti, Albizzi, Medici and Pazzi who used their wealth to influence elections. The city saw many bitter and violent family feuds. The success of one family often led to their rivals being driven into exile.

5 This painting from the Palazzo Vecchio (Old Palace) in Florence shows the ruling council at work. It was painted by Giorgio Vasari and shows the council discussing a war with Pisa in 1494.

1 What sort of men are those in source 5 – working men, men of the 'middling kind', or the well-born?

2 How good a source for Florentine politics in 1400 would you expect Leonardo Bruni (source 6) to be?

3 In what ways do source 5 and Bruni's description of Florentine politics agree or conflict with the previous information you have been given?

7 The Medici Palace in Florence as seen from the street.

The writer and politician Leonardo Bruni (1370–1444) who was the Chancellor (senior government official) in the 1430s wrote this about his city:

6 The Florentine republic is neither completely aristocratic [run by nobles] nor completely popular [run by the people] but is a mixture of both forms . . . it accepts men of the middling kind – or rather, it tends to the well-born and richer kind of men provided that they are not excessively powerful.

Leonardo Bruni, *The Florentine Republic*, 1439

The Medici

Cosimo de' Medici, 1389–1464

The building shown in sources 7 and 8 still stands in the centre of Florence, a short walk northwards from the cathedral. Cosimo de'Medici had the architect Michelozzo design it in 1446. He had already turned down a design by another architect, Brunelleschi, because it was too showy. In the chapel of the palace is the picture (source 9) of the Magi, or Three Wise Men. It

8 The inside courtyard of the Medici Palace. The Medici coat of arms is placed above each arch.

4 What do sources 7, 8 and 9 tell you about Cosimo de' Medici?

is also a portrait of Cosimo (on the white horse), his sons, grandsons and household.

Cosimo was the richest man in Florence and possibly in the whole of Europe. His father, Giovanni, had made a fortune out of wool and banking. He had become the banker of the Pope, who was the head of the Church, and set up branches of the Medici bank all over Europe. Cosimo was as skilful a businessman as his father, but much more active in politics.

In 1433 the most powerful family in Florence was the Albizzi. It led the city into war against the neighbouring town of Lucca. Cosimo opposed the war and the angry Albizzi, having failed to get him executed, banished him to Venice. The war against Lucca went badly and friends of the Medici whipped up popular feeling against the Albizzi. In 1434 Cosimo returned home in triumph. It was the Albizzi's turn to be banished. From then on Cosimo was the most powerful man in Florence. Aeneas Sylvius, Bishop of Siena and later to become Pope Pius II, wrote in 1458:

10 Political questions are settled in his [Cosimo's] house. The man he chooses holds office . . . He it is who decides peace and war . . . He is King in everything but name.

Quoted by C. Hibbert, *The Rise and Fall of the House of Medici*, 1974

The Florentines liked their apparently free elections and disliked anyone who seemed to be getting too big for his boots. So Cosimo pretended to be an

9 A detail of the *Procession of the Magi*, painted by Benozzo Gozzoli on a wall of the chapel of the Medici Palace in 1459.

1 How powerful do sources 10 and 11 suggest Cosimo was?

2 Note down the writers of sources 10 and 11 and their occupations. How well-informed were they likely to be about Cosimo's power?

3 How, according to the Venetian ambassador, did Cosimo win back his popularity in 1454?

ordinary citizen. He did not often hold public office and he gave the impression of being a modest private man of business.

Cosimo controlled the city by using his wealth to make sure that those who could vote voted for his friends and family. He also used his wealth in other ways to keep the people on his side, as the Venetian ambassador reported in 1454:

> **11** In order to retain popular favour, Cosimo has had to give out many bushels [measures] of corn every day to the poor who were crying out and grumbling because of the rise in prices.
>
> Quoted by C. Hibbert *The Rise and Fall of the House of Medici*, 1974

He kept his most dangerous enemies in exile and weakened his rivals by making them pay heavy taxes. But he was also a wise ruler. He paid for fine buildings and other works of art. He gave generously to charities. When he died in 1464, the government gave him the title 'Pater Patriae' (Father of the Country) which was carved on his tomb.

Cosimo's son, Piero, succeeded him as head of the family. Piero's health was poor (he was nicknamed 'the Gouty') and he only lived until 1469. He was succeeded by his son, Lorenzo, a young man of twenty.

Lorenzo de' Medici, 1449–92

Lorenzo was clever and charming, a fine poet and sportsman, arrogant and ugly but with an unusual gift for friendship. He used his money to lay on entertainments like tournaments and parades, and to bring the best artists and writers to work in Florence. Lorenzo himself wrote poetry and a famous poem he wrote goes:

> **12** How beautiful is youth, which is soon over and gone; let him who would be happy, seize the moment; for tomorrow may never come.

Lorenzo was a poor businessman. He liked spending, but left the business to managers who did not do a good job. The London, Bruges and Milan branches of the Medici bank all failed during his lifetime and his income came more from land and from city taxes than from trade.

Like his father and grandfather, Lorenzo played a leading part in Florentine politics. He did so, he said, with reluctance, partly because he was asked to and partly:

> **14** In order to protect our friends and property; since it fares ill in Florence with anyone who is rich but does not have any share in government.

13 The title page from a book of songs by Lorenzo de' Medici. This edition was published in 1568.

Lorenzo controlled the city in much the same way as Cosimo and he never held high office himself. Instead he used his wealth and family connections to make sure that the government of the city did what he wanted. He was known as 'the Magnificent', but, in fact, this title was given to the head of any noble family at that time.

Sometimes he would ignore the wishes of the elected government of Florence, as the neighbouring town of Volterra learnt to its cost in 1472. After a dispute about an alum mine and a riot in the town centre, Lorenzo, without the agreement of the Florentine government, sent an army into Volterra which plundered it and murdered hundreds of women and men.

In 1478 he nearly lost his life in the so-called Pazzi conspiracy. Members of the Pazzi family, supported by Pope Sixtus IV, planned to stab Lorenzo and his brother, Giuliano, to death at Mass in Florence cathedral. They killed Giuliano, but only wounded Lorenzo who managed to rally his supporters. In five days of street violence eighty-five relatives and friends of the Pazzi family were hanged without trial and their bodies left dangling in the streets.

The Pazzi conspiracy was part of a wider anti-Florence move led by the Pope and the King of Naples. As a result, from 1478 to 1480, the city was in a weak position politically. However, Lorenzo was a brave and skilful politician. He won the respect of most of the other Italian rulers and saved his city from disaster. He worked hard to prevent Italy being harmed by more destructive wars and his early death in 1492, aged only forty-three, was a setback to the whole Italian peninsula. Thirty years later, Niccolo Machiavelli, a Florentine official and political thinker, wrote:

15 All the princes of Italy mourned his death . . . all the bad seeds of war began to sprout which, not long after, he who could quell [crush] them being no longer alive, ruined and are still ruining Italy.

N. Machiavelli, *History of Florence*, 1525

Giovanni (1360–1429) = Piccarda Bueri

Cosimo (1389–1464) = Contessina de Bardi

Piero (the Gouty) (1416–69) = Lucrezia Tornabuoni

Lorenzo (the Magnificent) (1449–92) = Clarice Orsini

Piero (1471–1503) = Alfonsina Orsini

16 The Medici Family Tree
(1360–1503).

4 **Down the left-hand side of a page, make a time-line which begins in 1400 and ends in 1500. Divide it into ten-year intervals. Put on it in the correct places: a) Cosimo's triumph over the Albizzi, b) the death of Cosimo, c) the death of Piero the Gouty, d) Lorenzo's attack on Volterra, e) the Pazzi conspiracy, and f) the death of Lorenzo.**

5 **To the right of your time-line, add two further columns. Head the first 'political skill' and the second 'business success'. Write comments under both these headings against the periods when Cosimo and Lorenzo were head of the family.**

6 **Explain how Cosimo and Lorenzo controlled Florence without being part of the government.**

17 The cloister of the monastery of San Marco. The architect of this building was Michelozzo.

Patrons

The reason why the Medici family is so important to the Italian Renaissance is because members of the family were the best patrons in Florence. Patrons are people who ask artists to work for them and pay them for their work.

Cosimo was the most generous patron of all. He paid scholars to study Greek philosophy and to collect books from ancient Greece and Rome. He spent immense sums on monasteries and churches, on his family palace and on his country villas. The Monastery of San Marco meant much to him. He spent hundreds of thousands of florins on rebuilding it. When the monks protested that he was being too generous, he said:

18 Never shall I be able to give to God enough to set him down in my books as a debtor.

Quoted by C. Hibbert, *The Rise and Fall of the House of Medici*, 1974

Cosimo's grandson, Lorenzo, was much loved by poets and writers, who he invited to his country villas to talk and to relax. He gave generously to the University of Florence, encouraged such artists as Botticelli and Michelangelo (see pages 16 to 17), and built up a superb collection of books and precious stones.

Other merchant families, like the Rucellai and the Pazzi, followed the Medici example and added fine buildings to the city. Giovanni Rucellai was ready to pay for such projects because, he said:

19 . . . they have given me the greatest pleasure, because in part they serve the honour of God, as well as of the city, and act as a memorial to myself.

G. Rucellai, *Memoirs*, 1473

20 The Medici villa at Poggio a Caiano, one of Lorenzo's country houses outside Florence, where he gardened, kept pigs and entertained his friends. The house was built in the 1480s.

The rich guilds (associations of craftspeople) were also important patrons. The Wool Guild put the architect Brunelleschi in charge of building the cathedral dome and the Cloth Guild paid the sculptor Ghiberti for the doors of the baptistery.

In 1425 the consuls (officers) of the Wool Guild met to discuss its failure to win the prize for the best statue for a church in the centre of Florence. It had come third to the Cloth and Banking Guilds. They decided at their meeting:

21 For the splendour and honour of the Guild, the lord consuls desire to put this matter right . . . they will construct a statue of the blessed Stephen . . . which will exceed or at least equal in beauty and decoration the more beautiful ones [already in place]. In the construction of this statue . . . the lord consuls may spend up to 1,000 florins.

Consuls of the Wool Guild, *Deliberations*, 1425

Ghiberti, who was then the most fashionable sculptor in Florence, was given the work.

Many churches had their own clubs or confraternities which raised money for charity and also employed artists to work for the church. In Florence, as elsewhere in Italy, there was great popular interest in art so most people with money to spare were keen to act as patrons.

1 Note for each of sources 17, 21 and 22 a) the name of the patron, b) the result of his spending, and c) the artist who gained the work.
2 What reasons do Cosimo de' Medici and Giovanni Rucellai give for their readiness to spend so much money? Which do you think was the most powerful reason?
3 What was the main reason of the Wool Guild (source 21) for paying for a statue of St Stephen? Why did it choose Ghiberti to carve the statue?
4 What does source 21 tell us about Florentine attitudes to art and design?

22 The new front of the Church of Santa Maria Novella, designed by Leon Alberti and paid for by Giovanni Rucellai.

Review and Assessment

Lorenzo de' Medici: for and against

Lorenzo de' Medici was the most powerful man in Florence from 1469 to 1492. He was a generous patron of artists and writers, and most history books describe the time when he was in power as a golden age. However, as you know, the Pazzi family tried to murder him and many others disliked him and his ways. Read these sources and decide what you think of him.

The painter and writer, Giorgio Vasari had nothing but praise for him:

> **23** In the time of Lorenzo de' Medici ... which was truly a golden age for men of intelligence, an artist, Allessandro Botticelli ... gave up painting and having no income to live on fell into very great distress ... If Lorenzo, for whom he had once done some work, had not helped him ... he would almost have died of hunger.
>
> Vasari, *Lives*, 1550

> **24** Lorenzo decided that he would ... help the young Michelangelo [who grew up to become the greatest of all the sculptors of the Renaissance] ... He gave him a room at the Palazzo Medici ... Michelangelo ate at Lorenzo's table with the sons of the family, and Lorenzo always treated him with the greatest respect ...
>
> Vasari, *Lives*, 1550

Machiavelli also thought well of him:

> **25** Lorenzo made the city larger and more beautiful ... and kept it in a state of feasting and tournaments ... He was particularly dear to Fortune and to God ... Never did a man die who had such a reputation for wisdom and who was so greatly mourned by his native city.
>
> Machiavelli, *History of Florence*, 1525

There were other opinions; for example, Alemanno Rinuccini, a noble who lived in Florence at the same time as Lorenzo and knew him well, declared:

> **26** He was an evil and cruel tyrant.
>
> Rinuccini, *Dialogue on Liberty*, 1497

The fiery preacher Girolamo Savonarola, who was Prior of St Mark's and met Lorenzo a number of times, also thought badly of him:

27 If a tyrant [he is meaning here Lorenzo] seems modest and friendly, he is in fact being devilishly clever, making himself out to be an angel of light in order to do greater harm. Tyrants are too proud and listen to flatterers. They demand unfair taxes, oppress the poor . . . and bribe voters.

G. Savonarola, preaching in Florence in 1491

1 From these sources, note a) two facts about Lorenzo, b) one point of view in his favour, and c) one point of view against him.

2   **a** If you only had sources 23, 24 and 25 what would be your opinion of Lorenzo as a ruler?
  b If you only had sources 26 and 27, what would be your opinion then?

3 Vasari wrote source 23 nearly sixty years after Lorenzo's death. Macchiavelli was still a young man when Lorenzo died and wrote his book (source 25) for Lorenzo's nephew. Both Rinuccini and Savonarola were political opponents of Lorenzo in the last years of his life.

Comment on the strengths and weaknesses of each of those sources as evidence of Lorenzo's achievements.

4 Does it surprise you that it is the later writers who look back to Lorenzo's time as a golden age while those who lived at the same time had a much lower opinion? Why?

5 Re-read pages 12–14. Make two lists a) of Lorenzo's achievements, and b) of his mistakes and failures.

6 In your judgement, how good a ruler of Florence was Lorenzo? Was he better or worse than his grandfather Cosimo de' Medici?

2 The Florentine Renaissance

Some Florentine artists of the early Renaissance

Florence had been famous for many years for the beauty of its buildings and the skill of its craftspeople. It had already produced fine painters like Giotto (c.1267–1337) and great poets like Dante (1265–1321). However, the fifteenth century was the golden age of Florence. Never before nor since has one city produced so many brilliant artists in so short a time. You have already been introduced to some of them in Chapter 1.

Filippo Brunelleschi (1377–1466) and architecture

The dome (*duomo*) of Florence cathedral dominates the city's skyline to this day. That dome is Brunelleschi's masterpiece. How he designed it and the success of his design tells us much not only about Brunelleschi himself but about the careful thought which the Florentines gave to their public buildings.

In 1400 the state of the cathedral embarrassed the city. Large and handsomely decorated in white and coloured marble, it lacked a dome. Its first architect had died leaving an open space so huge that the largest dome made since Roman times was needed to cover it. No-one could work out how to build it. The Clothmakers' Guild, which was responsible for completing the building, discussed endlessly how the problem might be solved. Eventually, in 1420, it called together some of the best architects from Italy and from other countries to compete against each other to find the best solution.

Among the competitors was Filippo Brunelleschi, small, bouncy and confident, with many good buildings already to his name. He had worked out years earlier how the dome could be built, but refused to show his plans to anyone because he was afraid that they might be used by his rivals.

The best source we have for the artistic achievements of the Italian Renaissance is a book by Giorgio Vasari, himself a Florentine painter of the sixteenth century (see page 10). It is called the *Lives of the Most Eminent Painters, Sculptors and Architects* and was written between 1546 and 1548. In it Vasari tells how Brunelleschi won the competition:

1 He proposed to the architects . . . that whoever could make an egg stand upright on a flat piece of marble should build the dome . . . Taking an egg therefore, all the masters [architects] tried to make it stand upright, but no-one could find a way. Whereupon Filippo, being told to make it stand, took it graciously, and giving one end a blow on the flat piece of marble, made it stand upright. The architects protested that they could have done the same; but Filippo answered, laughing, that they could have made the dome, if they had seen his design.

Vasari, *Lives of the Most Eminent Painters, Sculptors and Architects,* published 1550

2 **A modern photograph of the Duomo in Florence.**

3 A diagram of the internal construction of the Duomo.

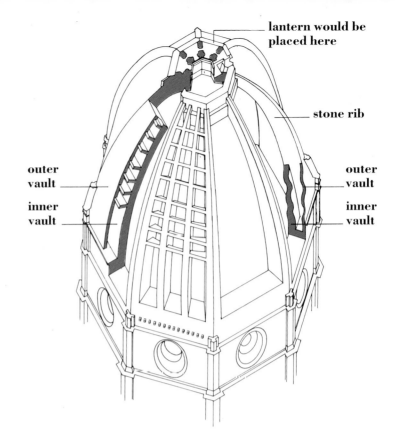

lantern would be placed here

stone rib

outer vault

inner vault

outer vault

inner vault

Brunelleschi was appointed and work began under his supervision in 1420. He explained his design in a note to the Clothmakers' Guild:

4 I find that it is in no way possible to raise the dome perfectly round, seeing the surface above, where the lantern [the small stone tower at the very top which lets in the light] is to go would be so great that the laying of any weight on it would soon destroy it . . . so I have decided to turn the inner part of the vault in pointed sections . . . so that when it is loaded with the lantern, both will unite to make the vaulting strong . . . Then on the other side there must be another vault to protect the inner one from the rain.

Quoted in Vasari, *Lives of the Artists*, 1550

The dome was finished, except for the lantern, sixteen years later in 1436. The lantern was finally added after Brunelleschi's death.

Brunelleschi was a gifted sculptor as well as an architect, but in 1402 he had lost a sculpture competition to his hated rival, Lorenzo Ghiberti (see page 22). From then on he concentrated entirely on architecture. Like the cathedral dome, his other major works (churches, palaces and a hospital) were built in Florence. With his friend Donatello he paid a long visit to Rome where he made many sketches of the ancient ruins. In his opinion the architecture of ancient Rome was far better than the medieval (Gothic) style which in 1400 was still the fashionable style all over Europe. His ambition was to break completely with this 'Gothic' style and to create buildings which the ancient Romans would have admired. He made this break successfully and set the architecture of Europe on a new course.

5 Brunelleschi's Hospital of the Innocents.

Donatello (1386–1466) and sculpture

One of Brunelleschi's closest friends was Donatello, the finest sculptor of his generation. Donatello was born in Florence and lived until he was eighty. He produced many sculptures in wood and bronze as well as in stone. Though he spent most of his life in Florence, he worked in other Italian cities and had a great influence on younger sculptors. He did some important work in Padua (see page 29) whose citizens showered him with so much praise that he returned with relief to Florence, since he found the lively criticism of his home town much more to his taste.

Donatello was a kind and generous man, even at the height of his fame. He kept the money he earned in a basket in his studio to be shared by his workmen and his friends. However, he had no doubt about the quality of his work. When a merchant from Genoa claimed that he was charging too high a price for a bronze head he had made, Donatello simply pushed the bronze off a balcony into the street below and walked off saying that the merchant was more used to bargaining for beans than for statues. His statues are very realistic and somehow manage to give a strong sense of human feeling.

Masaccio (1401–c.1428) and painting

Another friend of Brunelleschi was the absent-minded Masaccio. He became so involved in his painting that he bothered little about practical things like clothing and money. His most important works were wall-paintings in the Brancacci Chapel in Florence. Though he died while still in his twenties, his style was so new and so powerful that it greatly impressed the next generation of up-and-coming painters. His special interest and skill was to give to his paintings a strong sense of three dimensions. This means that objects and people in them do not appear flat, but look more rounded and life-like.

6 Donatello's *Mary Magdalen.*

7 *The Tribute Money,* **painted by Masaccio.**

8 Ghiberti's Gates of Paradise.

Ghiberti (1378–1455) and the baptistery doors

Not all the artists of Florence were Brunelleschi's friends. One he strongly disliked was Lorenzo Ghiberti who beat both Donatello and himself in a competition in 1402. The prize was to make new bronze doors for the baptistery, one of Florence's oldest buildings. So successful were Ghiberti's first set of doors that, once they were finished, he was asked to do a second pair. These he only finished in 1452, three years before his death.

Both pairs of doors are very skilfully made but the second pair are more adventurous and show the advances which Florentine art had made in the early years of the fifteenth century. Another great Florentine sculptor, Michelangelo, called them the Gates of Paradise, a name which has stuck to this day.

1 What do these people do: a) an architect, b) a sculptor, c) a painter, d) a craftsperson?
2 Put the correct occupation and place against each person:

Brunelleschi	sculptor	baptistery doors
Donatello	painter	cathedral dome
Ghiberti	architect	Brancacci Chapel
Masaccio	sculptor	Padua

3 From the pictures you have seen so far, describe the subjects which Florentine painters and sculptors usually showed.
4 Who paid these artists' fees?

What exactly was the Renaissance in Florence?

As you have seen, there were many brilliant artists in early fifteenth-century Florence. However, it was not just the number of artists which made the Renaissance. There was an especially new outlook on life among educated Florentines which made them highly confident about themselves and the future. This general cheerful confidence affected the artists too, and helped to make their work so attractive.

The new interest in ancient Greece and Rome

The Medici, their friends and many other Florentines believed that they were living at the dawn of a new age. They were doing better, they thought, than earlier generations and much better than other parts of Europe.

9 *Mars and Venus* **by Sandro Botticelli. Botticelli took two ancient Roman gods as the subject of this painting.**

The key to their success, they were sure, was their knowledge of the 'classical age' of ancient Greece and Rome. The Florentines studied classical languages and history very keenly and thought that they understood ancient Greece and Rome better than anyone else. They believed that they were able to learn lessons from that classical past which would improve their own lives.

When the Roman Empire collapsed between AD450 and 550, almost the only places where books survived were monasteries. So, one Florentine Renaissance hobby was hunting for 'classical' books in Latin and Greek in monasteries all over Europe. One particularly keen book-hunter was Poggio Bracciolini who, while working for the Pope, hunted through England and Switzerland as well as Italy in search of neglected classical books. He wrote in great excitement to a friend in 1417 when he found a book by the Latin author Quintilian in the Swiss monastery of St Gall:

10 We found it safe and sound, though filthy with mould and dust . . . in a sort of foul and gloomy dungeon at the bottom of one of the towers.

Poggio Bracciolini, letter to Guarino Guarini, 1417

The best-educated Florentines became as keen on Greek as on Latin. Chrysolaras, a teacher from Constantinople, gave Greek classes in Florence from 1397 to 1400. He brought with him many books which previously had not been well-known in Italy. The ideas of the great classical Greek philosopher Plato (428–348 BC) became fashionable.

Humanism

Source 11 is a drawing by Florence's best painter, Leonardo da Vinci. It illustrates the idea of the Greek philosopher Protagoras that 'man is the measure of all things'; that is, human beings are the centre of the world; through the human mind comes the understanding of our world; and through the proportions of the human body we gain our sense of beauty and good design.

What the Florentines liked about the classical way of thinking was its confidence in human beings. If people had the skill and the personality, the people of ancient Greece and Rome believed, they could do great things. Following the teachings of their church leaders, Europeans of the Middle Ages had thought differently. They believed that men and women were sinful beings who could achieve nothing worthwhile without the help of God.

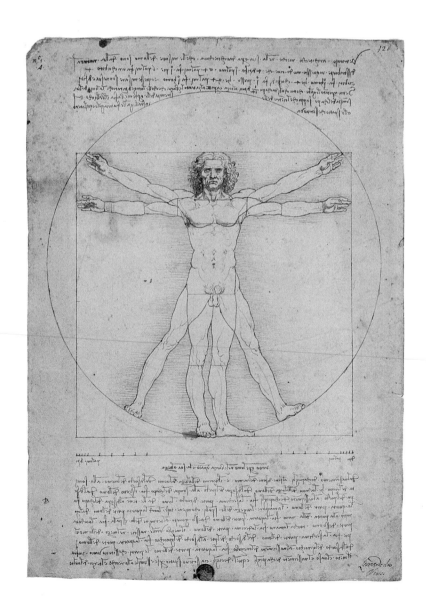

11 *Everyman* by Leonardo da Vinci. It shows the proportions of the human body.

The name 'humanism' is given to the new interest in the world of Greece and Rome, and to the renewed confidence in what human beings could achieve by their own efforts. 'Humanists' were those who shared these ideas. They thought they were bringing to life again all that was best about the classical world and, in that sense, they were helping in a rebirth or renaissance.

The humanists' interest in the classical world brought important changes to education. Previously almost all schools were church schools. The main subjects taught were religion and Church Latin, which was in many ways different to the Latin of the ancient world.

Now, classical works were providing new ideas about education. In 1411, Guarino Guarini, friend of the book-hunting Poggio Bracciolini, translated *On Educating Children* by the Greek writer Plutarch. In fact, the book by Quintilian which Poggio himself discovered in 1417 in the monastery of St Gall (see page 23) was also about education.

The Duke of Mantua, a city in the Po valley between Florence and Venice, founded a school there in 1423 and appointed Vittorino da Feltre as its first teacher. Vittorino started just with the three sons of the duke, but by the time of his death in 1446 he had increased its numbers to about seventy. Most pupils came from noble families, but there were some poorer children too. Vittorino charged fees according to the family's means and sometimes paid for the poorer pupils himself.

Vittorino believed that learning should, wherever possible, be enjoyable, and named the school building 'La Gioiosa' or Happy House. He wanted the school to be an active Christian community and began each day with a religious service.

In Vittorino's school, the most important subjects were Latin and Greek, firmly based on the writers of the ancient world. From their study of classical writings pupils learnt about ancient history and politics. They also took mathematics and astronomy. Games were an important part of the curriculum; notably leaping, running and ball-games.

This humanist approach to education was liked by many noble families and also rich merchants. In Florence Leon Alberti, who is now best known as an architect (see page 15), wrote this in 1435:

12 I have never liked the common saying of some people that if you know how to sign your name and can figure out your balance, you have enough education.

Leon Alberti, *Della Famiglia* [On the Family], 1435

He suggested that good fathers should make sure their children read a wide range of Latin and Greek writers and take part in archery and ball-games.

13 **Head of a victorious athlete sculpted in c.AD 130.**

14 **The inside of the Pantheon in Rome which was built in AD 120.**

15 **A Roman sculpture of the Emperor Marcus Aurelius, carved in c.AD 180.**

The Renaissance in the arts

The Renaissance changed first Italy and then Europe in many different ways. The fastest and most noticeable changes were in the arts – architecture, painting and sculpture.

The artists of the Gothic period (c.1200–1400 in Italy, c.1200–1500 elsewhere in Europe) worked to glorify God. Their buildings with their pointed arches had a strong upward thrust towards heaven. Their statues and paintings also drew the eye upward and aimed to give an impression of majesty or dignity, to be larger than life rather than realistic.

The artists of ancient Rome worked to impress men not God. Their well-proportioned, round-arched and many-columned buildings were grand rather than pretty, solid rather than inspiring. Their best sculptors were excellent craftsmen who produced realistic shapes, but of perfect men and women rather than of individuals with their own particular personalities.

The artists of the Renaissance worked to the human scale, using the idea that 'man is the measure of all things', to make the present world as attractive to live in as possible. They were strongly affected by Roman examples. Renaissance architects preferred round arches and designed their buildings so that the measurements of important features of the building – e.g. length, height, size of windows – were carefully calculated.

For example, Brunelleschi's designs for the Hospital of the Innocents (see page 20) are based mathematically on cubes and semi-circles. The distance between the centres of the columns is exactly the same as the distance between the columns and the wall of the building itself. The builders of the hospital complained about all the measurements he gave them! Brunelleschi believed that from the mathematical relationships which he had calculated came a well-proportioned and attractive building. Compared to Roman buildings, Renaissance ones often have a lightness and an inventiveness all of their own.

Like Roman sculptors, Renaissance sculptors aimed to be realistic but they also succeeded in capturing in their carvings a sense of individual personalities. Donatello's *Gattamelata* (see page 29) is not especially handsome or heroic. Rather, he appears as very determined, but with a trace of sadness about him, perhaps from having fought in so many wars. '

Renaissance painters had few surviving classical paintings to study so they were less influenced by classical models. Like Renaissance sculptors, they wished to be as realistic as possible and, like the architects, became very interested in the ways mathematics could help them. They were particularly keen to make their two-dimensional pictures more realistic by seeming three-dimensional. To achieve this they found the mathematics of perspective particularly useful.

To help you to understand the idea of perspective, imagine you are standing on a broad straight highway which runs across open country to the horizon. As you look into the distance, the road narrows into nothingness. The further things are from you the smaller they seem. A painter would use his knowledge of perspective to draw that highway narrowing to nothing just as it would appear to the naked eye. By using this method, two-dimensional pictures gain the third dimension of space and seem more realistic.

Led by Brunelleschi, the artists of Renaissance Florence became very excited by the effects of perspective. Masaccio's *Trinity* (see page 28), which draws your eye into an apparently large space behind the crucified Christ, is a good example of the use of perspective.

16 **A sculpture from Chartres Cathedral, carved in the early thirteenth century.**

17 *Madonna and Child*, **painted by Cimabùe in 1280.**

18 **The inside of the church of Santa Maria Novella, built in 1279.**

19 The inside of the church of Santo Spirito, designed by Brunelleschi in 1434.

20 *The Trinity*, painted by Masaccio in 1427.

21 *Gattamelata* in Padua, sculpted by Donatello in about 1450.

Why did the Renaissance begin in Florence?

Fifteenth-century Florence produced more outstanding works of art than any city in history. It is difficult to explain exactly why but one important cause was the wealth and confidence of its leading citizens. They had money to spend and enjoyed spending it on works of art.

Another reason was that there were good artists around who knew that people thought well of them in an enthusiastic and critical way, and that if they had talent they could make a decent living. Thanks to the standards set by the guilds over many years, artists and craftspeople aimed at the highest quality in their work.

Perhaps the most important reason of all was the mood of the city. The Florentines were proud of themselves. Perhaps because of the threat from Milan, they were particularly proud of their freedom from tyrants. They also looked to the future with confidence and were ready to try out new ideas.

For all these reasons the Medicean period in Florence was artistically remarkable.

1 Look closely at sources 14, 18 and 19. Explain which two are most alike and which is the Gothic building.
2 Do the same with the styles of sources 15, 16, and 21 and explain which is the Renaissance sculpture.
3 Look at sources 17 and 20. Which is the Gothic painting and which the Renaissance one?
4 What have the Renaissance examples 19, 20 and 21 got in common? How are they different from the Gothic examples 16, 17 and 18?
5 Brunelleschi thought that the Gothic style was awful. Four hundred years later, some of the leading art critics of England thought Renaissance designs bad and wanted cities to be rebuilt in the Gothic style. Which style to you prefer? Why?

Review and Assessment

The wealth, confidence and artistic brilliance of Renaissance Florence

22 This Florentine engraving of the fifteenth century shows a street scene.

1
  a How many different activities can you find in source 22?

  b What evidence is there in source 22 that Florence was a centre of learning, and of arts and crafts?

  c The main activities which made Florence wealthy are not shown in source 22. What were they?

  d In what style is the three-arched building in the middle distance? Who might have designed it?

2
Coluccio Salutati, Chancellor of Florence from 1375 to 1406, wrote of Florence:

23 What city, not merely in Italy but in the whole world, is stronger within its walls, prouder in its palaces, richer in its temples, more lovely in its buildings . . . Where is there trade richer in its variety? Where are there more famous men?

C. Salutati, *Letters*, c.1399

a When Salutati wrote this, Florence faced a dangerous threat. From whom?
b About what of Florence was he particularly proud? About what of today's Britain might a British Prime Minister be especially proud?
c What does source 23 tell you about Florentine attitudes to the arts?

3 Giovanni Rucellai, a merchant prince whose fortune was based on the dyeing industry, wrote in his *Memoirs* in 1473:

24 I have spent a great deal of money on my house and on the front of the church of Santa Maria Novella and on the chapel with the tomb I have made in the church of San Pancrazio . . .

G. Rucellai, *Memoirs*, 1473

a What is the name given to people who spend money employing artists?
b For what reasons was Rucellai ready to spend a great deal of money on the arts?
c Give other examples of individuals or groups in Florence who were prepared to spend money on the arts.

4 When Vasari asked himself why Florence came to produce so many brilliant artists, he gave this as the main reason:

25 the spirit of criticism; the air of Florence making minds naturally free, and not content with the second-rate.

Vasari, *Lives*, 1550

a Why should the spirit of criticism and freedom help artists to reach high standards?
b What evidence is there from the lives of Brunelleschi, Donatello and Ghiberti that criticism and freedom were important to them?
c Is there any evidence that competition was important too?

5 Write an essay explaining why the Italian Renaissance began in Florence. You should include as causes the following and show how they were connected:

trade; wealth and patronage; the city's pride in its achievements; the atmosphere of freedom; criticism and competition; and the determination of Brunelleschi, Donatello and Masaccio to revive the classical style.

Add other causes which you think worth mentioning and explain which of all these causes you believe to be the most important.

3 The Spread of the Renaissance in Italy

Renaissance ideas soon spread from Florence to other parts of Italy, particularly to the wealthy northern cities of Venice and Milan.

Venice

1 **Imagine that the year is 1450 and you are a traveller visiting Venice for the first time. You hire a boat to bring you across the lagoon from the mainland and to take you along the Grand Canal (the waterway shaped like a back-to-front S). You end up in St Mark's Square, the large open space in the centre of the city.**
a) What would you have found unusual about Venice?
b) What would you have seen which made you think that the city was rich and powerful and that the city's wealth came from trade with distant lands?

1 A drawing of Venice during the fifteenth century.

Venice was larger, richer and more powerful than Florence. Its population numbered 100,000. In 1423 its Doge (or Duke) Tommaso Mocenigo could boast that it made a profit of 4 million ducats each year from its exports and imports. It controlled the large island of Crete and held many other important trading posts in the Eastern Mediterranean. The Venetians believed that because of its wealth and military strength, their city was equal to or more powerful than any nation in Europe, except France. They were probably right.

2 **Venice's position on the trade-routes of Europe and the Eastern Mediterranean in the early fifteenth century.**

KEY
Venice and Venetian territory
Trade routes through Venice
• City

0 100 200 KM

1 **Why was Venice better placed than Milan or Florence to control the trade between Europe and the East?**

2 **In what sort of goods did Venetian merchants trade to bring wealth to themselves and to the city?**

Certainly visitors from northern Europe were amazed by its appearance. An English priest who visited it for the first time in the last years of the fourteenth century wrote that 'all the things which make a city glorious are better in Venice than all places I have ever seen', while a century later a French visitor, Philippe de Commines, described the Grand Canal as 'the fairest and best-built street in the world.'

Venice had been powerful for centuries. It had grown fast as a trading city during the Middle Ages and by the end of the fourteenth century had defeated Genoa, its main Italian trading rival. Its power was built on its control of the trade between western and central Europe and the eastern Mediterranean and Asia. Venetian merchants profitably exchanged a huge variety of goods like the wool of England and the cloth of Flanders for the sugar of Cyprus, the spices of the Far East and and the pearls of Ceylon. Its great Arsenal (which you can see on the right edge of source 1) built a stream of warships to defend its trading empire. Although in the east the Ottoman Turks were a growing threat, the Venetians still held the upper hand, defeating them in a major sea-battle near Gallipoli in 1416.

How was Venice governed?

Venice was an oligarchy; that is a state ruled by only a few. The few were 2,500 noblemen, aged twenty-five or more, who attended the Great Council which chose the smaller committees that carried out the work of government. Much day-to-day business was done by a Senate of 300. A very powerful Council of Ten looked after defence, finance and the secret police. The Ten had a fearsome reputation since they dealt swiftly and ruthlessly with people who they thought were enemies of the state.

The Doge was the elected head of state and had a large say in political matters as long as the Ten and Senate backed him. The Venetians prided themselves on the fact that their Doge, unlike other Italian rulers, could never become a tyrant and rule as he liked. In comparison with Florence, which as a result of family rivalries had frequent changes of government, riots, murders and banishments, the Venetian government was calm, efficient and unchanging. Marino Sanudo, the city's official historian in the early sixteenth century, could write:

3 This holy republic is governed with such order that it is a marvellous thing. She has neither popular riots nor fighting between her noble families, but all unite in making her greater; and therefore, as wise men say, she will last for ever.

M. Sanudo, *The Diaries*, published in Venice in 1879

On sea or on land: where did the future lie?

Though Doge Mocenigo could boast about his city's wealth and strength in the 1420s, he worried about its future. He knew that many nobles wished to seize parts of the Italian mainland to prevent Milan from becoming too strong. Mocenigo was sure that the city's real strength came from the sea. He remembered a prophecy made two centuries earlier by St Joachim of Fiore that 'the Lion of St Mark [Venice] would suffer disasters if the sea was deserted for the land.'

Winning land would mean endless wars which Venice could not afford and, in the long-run, would lead to the collapse of the sea-based empire. Do not make Francesco Foscari Doge, Mocenigo warned from his deathbed, since Foscari would go to war to win an empire on the Italian mainland.

The electors ignored Mocenigo and made Foscari Doge. Foscari did go to war and gained much land (see map 5 below). His successors continued the expansion on the mainland, usually fighting with Florence against Milan.

4 Francesco Foscari. Painted by Lazzari Bastiani.

5 Venice's mainland gains.

KEY
- • City
- — Border
- ～ River

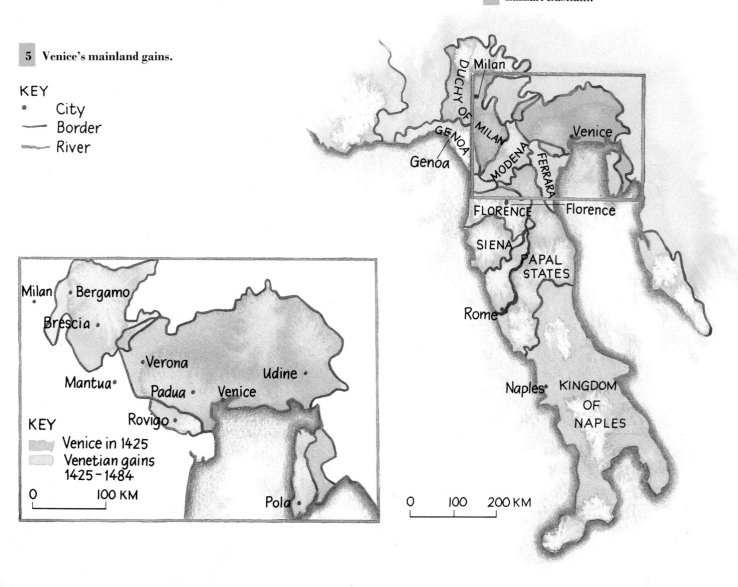

KEY

- Venice in 1425
- Venetian gains 1425–1484

0   100 KM

0   100   200 KM

1 **What is an oligarchy? Describe the ways in which the government of Venice differed from that of Florence.**
2 **What sort of empire did Venice have up to 1425? What sort of empire interested Doge Foscari? For what reasons?**
3 **When and for what reasons did Venice stop being one of the foremost trading cities of Europe?**

Mocenigo's warnings proved correct. In the wars which followed the invasion of Italy by the French in 1494, Venice faced many enemies because of the land which it had recently seized. Pope Julius II (see pages 45–46) persuaded the kings of France, Spain and Hungary to fight with him against the over-mighty city. At the battle of Agnadello in 1509, these allies heavily defeated the Venetian army.

Meanwhile, in the Eastern Mediterranean, the powerful and successful Muslim Turks advanced by both land and sea. In 1453 the historic Christian city of Constantinople (modern Istanbul) fell to them. Venetian forces fought in vain to defend Constantinople and then in a long war from 1463 to 1479 which ended with the loss of Euboea and the Morea (parts of modern Greece). From then on, hard though they tried, the Venetians could not stop the Turkish advance.

It was a cruel war. Neither side showed much mercy to captured sailors. When Euboea finally fell, the Turks slaughtered most of the Venetian inhabitants, including the women and children. As for the Venetian Governor who had surrendered on the promise that he would not have his head cut off, they cut him in half at the waist!

As the years passed, Venice ceased to be one of the leading trading cities of Europe. Between 1480 and 1520 Portuguese sailors opened up a new sea-route to India and the Far East. The countries with ports on Atlantic-facing coasts were much better placed to take advantage of the new trade-routes. When the news reached Venice that the Portuguese had successfully unloaded the first cargoes of eastern spices on the wharves of Lisbon, the merchants of Venice were badly shaken. 'The wisest heads,' said the banker Priuli, 'think it the worst piece of information we could possibly have had.'

Over the years Venetian traders lost out to those from Portugal, Spain, France, England and the Low Countries. However, with its industries, like glass-blowing and printing, it remained reasonably wealthy and, unlike the rest of Italy, kept its independence from foreign rule until the end of the eighteenth century.

The Renaissance in Venice

Venetians were well-educated by the standards of the time. They, like the Florentines, were attracted to humanist ideas and their many links with Greece gave them a particularly good knowledge of ancient Greek writers. Venice also became an important centre of printing and publishing (see page 61).

Though the Venetian empire grew weaker, the arts flourished, particularly painting, and, unlike the rest of Italy, continued to do so throughout the sixteenth century.

The Venetians were the first Italians to make much use of oil paints, which had been invented in the Low Countries. Vasari wrote about the

Venetian painter Antonello da Messina who had visited the Low Countries to study painting methods there:

> **6** Antonello did not leave the country until he had thoroughly mastered the method of colouring in oil . . . Not long after, he left Flanders [the Low Countries] to revisit his native country and to give Italy the benefit of this beautiful and useful secret . . . He went to Venice and made many oil paintings there, which are scattered about the houses of the nobles of the city, being much valued for their novelty.
>
> Vasari, *Lives*, 1550

Previously, up to about 1470, most Italian painters used 'tempera' paints made from colours blended with egg yolk and painted onto either wooden panels or damp lime-plastered walls. Oil paints which had the colours mixed with linseed oil gave an extra smoothness and richness. When you look at the Venetian paintings in this section, you should especially notice the warmth and richness of the colours, particularly of the clothing, and the way in which all the details are painted smoothly and precisely. The Venetians used oils on canvas as much as on wood.

Eric Newton, a twentieth-century art historian and critic compared Florentine and Venetian painting in this way:

> **8** To the Florentine, colour . . . was a quality to be added to design. To the Venetian it was inseparable [could not be separated] from design.
>
> E. Newton, *European Painting and Sculpture*, 1941

7 Antonello da Messina, *Portrait of a Man*, painted in about 1474.

4 What was the main difference between Florentine and Venetian Renaissance paintings?

9 Giovanni Bellini, *Doge Loredan.*

10 Giovanni Bellini, *Agony in the Garden.*

1 a) Where was oil painting invented?

b) How did Giovanni Bellini learn to use oils?

c) What difference did it make to a picture such as source 10?

2 a) (i) What fashion did Giovanni Bellini encourage Venetian noblemen to follow?

(ii) Give an example of this fashion.

b) Why did Vasari (source 11) approve of this fashion?

The Bellini family produced the leading Venetian painters of the fifteenth century – Jacopo (c.1405–70), the father, and his sons Gentile (1429–1507) and Giovanni (c.1430–1516). Jacopo had a good reputation in his lifetime and taught his more talented sons well.

The younger brother, Giovanni, was especially influenced by Antonello da Messina from whom he learnt about oil painting. He became famous for his portraits as well as for his religious works. Vasari described how portraits became fashionable:

11 Giovanni Bellini introduced into Venice the fashion that everyone should have his portrait painted by him or by some other master, wherefore in all the houses of Venice there are many portraits . . . a fashion which existed even among the ancients [of Rome] . . . to kindle [inspire] in the mind of their successors a love of excellence and of glory.

Vasari, *Lives*, 1550

Giovanni had a large workshop where assistants completed pictures under his supervision.

Gentile was a fine painter of city life and of portraits. His patrons included the religious confraternities (see page 15), one of which asked him to paint the picture below which gives an excellent idea of Venetian life. The government also gave him plenty of work. It employed him for many years decorating the Doge's palace and also sent him on a goodwill mission to the Turkish Sultan.

12 Gentile Bellini, *Procession of the Relic of the True Cross*. The procession is passing through St Mark's Square in Venice.

Although in the rest of Italy there were fewer talented painters during the sixteenth century, Venice, in contrast, continued to produce painters of high quality like Giorgione, Titian, Tintoretto, Veronese and the first female painter to become well-known, Sofonisba Anguissola.

Milan

Then, as now, Milan was one of the most important industrial centres in Italy and Europe. It lies on the northern edge of the fertile Po valley and controls two important trade-routes, one east-west from Venice to France, the other north-south from Germany to Florence and Rome. Its flourishing industries included arms, cloth and silk. With a population of 100,000, it was as large as Venice. It was also dangerous since its dukes were restlessly ambitious, wishing to rule as much of northern Italy as possible.

The Visconti and the Sforza

Using the information in the family tree (source 13):
3 List in chronological order all the Dukes of Milan, beginning with Giangaleazzo Visconti in 1378 and ending with Giangaleazzo Sforza in 1494.
4 Explain a) the relationship of Francesco Sforza to Filippo Maria Visconti, b) the relationship of Lodovico Sforza to Giangaleazzo Sforza, and c) how the French were able to claim in 1498 that Milan should be their's.
5 Who actually held power in Milan after 1480?

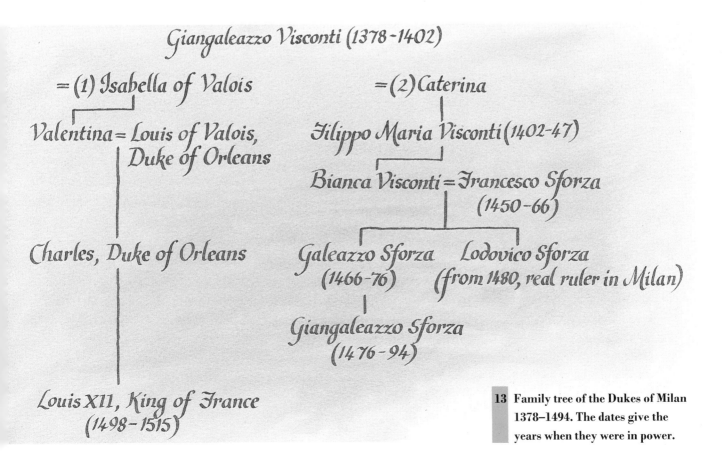

13 Family tree of the Dukes of Milan 1378–1494. The dates give the years when they were in power.

Lodovico Sforza may well have poisoned his nephew Giangaleazzo in 1494 so as to become duke himself. As a politician he was too clever by half. When the French invaded Italy in 1494, he began as their friend and then turned against them. When they invaded Italy again in 1499 he had to flee from Milan but was taken prisoner and died in a French prison in 1508. Like most of Italy, Milan then came under foreign rule.

Leonardo da Vinci in Milan

Lodovico had a magnificent court and was a generous patron to artists of all kinds. The most famous was Leonardo da Vinci who possessed the most varied and remarkable talents of all the artists of the Renaissance (see also Chapter 5).

Leonardo was born near Florence in 1452. His parents were not married. In fact, soon after his birth they married different partners. He grew up in his father's home and became an apprentice in the workshop of Verrocchio, one of the foremost artists of the Florence of Lorenzo de' Medici.

Handsome, intelligent with exceptional skill as a painter and musician, Leonardo won for himself a fine reputation while he was still in his twenties. He moved to Milan in 1482 and worked for Lodovico for seventeen years until the second French invasion of 1499.

In the letter which he wrote to Lodovico asking for work, he describes at length his skills as a military engineer and as a musician. He only mentions painting towards the end of the letter in one short sentence.

> **14** In times of peace . . . I can carry out in painting whatever may be done, as well as any other, be he who he may.
>
> Leonardo da Vinci, Letter to Lodovico Sforza, 1481

15 *Lady with an Ermine* **by Leonardo.**

However, he is best remembered today for his paintings and drawings, some excellent examples of which survive from his years in Milan. For example, the young lady in the portrait (source 15), now in a Polish museum, was Cecilia Gallerani, the lover of Lodovico.

The sketch (source 16) was one of many made for a colossal bronze statue of Lodovico's father, Francesco, on horseback. Leonardo eventually completed a clay model but it never got cast into bronze because Lodovico had to use the bronze which he had collected to make cannon. The clay model stood in a courtyard of the duke's palace for a few years until French soldiers destroyed it by using it for target practice.

16 One of Leonardo's drawings for the Sforza monument.

Leonardo and the *Last Supper*

Leonardo's most important painting in Milan is the *Last Supper*, painted on wall of the dining-room of the convent of Santa Maria della Grazie.

Matteo Bandello, who lived in Milan and knew Leonardo, tells us how Leonardo approached his work:

> **17** [Sometimes] he would come to the convent at early dawn . . . and work diligently until the shades of the evening made him cease, never thinking to take food at all, so absorbed was he in the work. At other times he would remain there three or four days without touching the picture, only coming for a few hours, with folded arms, to gaze at his figures . . .
>
> M. Bandello, *Novelle* [Tales], 1554

Vasari describes Leonardo working in the same way and adds how cross the Prior of the convent became:

> **18** The Prior of the convent continually nagged Leonardo to finish the work . . . and complained to the Duke who sent for Leonardo to inquire of his progress . . . Leonardo explained how men of genius really are doing most when they work least as they are thinking out ideas . . . the Duke declared that he was quite right and the poor Prior went back to his garden and left Leonardo in peace . . . The nobility of the painting made the King of France wish to take it home with him . . .
>
> Vasari, *Lives*, 1550

1 a) Why did the Prior complain to Duke Lodovico?
b) How did Leonardo defend himself?
c) Whose side did the Duke take?
2 What evidence is there that the painting was highly thought of once it was finished?

19 The *Last Supper* as it appears today, a dim shadow of how it looked when Leonardo finished it in 1497.

1 a) Why did the *Last Supper* decay?

b) If it is so badly decayed, why is it still worth so much attention?

2 Hartt in source 21 talks of the 'forms' and the 'space' of the picture. Study the picture carefully and describe firstly its forms and secondly its use of space.

However, it is probable that today we do not see the painting anywhere near to how it looked when it was first completed. It is the view of the art critic Kenneth Clark that:

> **20** ... we know that Leonardo used a medium containing oil and varnish. The wall was damp and as a result the painting very soon began to suffer ... It is hard to resist the conclusion that what we now see ... is largely the work of restorers.
>
> K. Clark, *Leonardo da Vinci*, 1939

Nonetheless the ruined painting still manages to impress. Another art critic, Ferdinand Hartt, writes:

> **21** Every silken curl, every passage of flesh must once have been perfect. Leonardo's forms have lost their definition, but not their impact, his space its precision [exact measurements] but not its depth. The psychological effect of the ruined masterpiece still brings the observer to silence.
>
> F. Hartt, *History of Italian Renaissance Art*, 1987

Rome

The early fifteenth century

A strange, sad place in 1400, Rome was quite different from the rich, lively, confident trading cities of northern Italy. A thousand years earlier it had been the greatest city the world had known with a million inhabitants and superb buildings spread across its seven hills. In 1400 it had fewer than 30,000 inhabitants. Some of the hills had gone back to nature and the ruins of ancient temples, palaces and public buildings were used as quarries. Rival noble families like the Colonna and the Orsini ran the city. Their quarrels went back generations and their gangs of supporters brawled in the streets.

To make matters worse, Rome could no longer claim to be the first city of Christianity. Ever since St Peter had been crucified there in the time of the Emperor Nero, Rome had been the capital of the Christian world. The successors of St Peter as bishops of Rome became known as the popes. Most Christians believed the pope to be the representative of God on earth and the leader of the Church. The Basilica (church) of St Peter, which stood on St Peter's grave, was the most important religious building in Europe and a popular place for pilgrims to visit. However, for most of the fourteenth century the popes lived in Avignon and, between 1378 and 1417, the Church was split between a pope in Rome, supported by Italians, and a pope in Avignon, supported by the French.

Rome did not stand on important trade-routes. To exist as a great city it needed to be a capital – the home of a government and its thousands of officials. Without a strong pope, it was a shadow of a city.

Rome as capital of the Church again

In 1417 the split in the Church was healed and the popes returned to Rome. The Vatican Palace alongside St Peter's Basilica was their home.

They wanted to be their own masters, to be free from having to depend on rulers like the kings of France and emperors of Germany for support. They also needed a steady income. For these reasons, the lands in central Italy known as the Papal States (see source 22) were important to them and they spent much time and energy in making sure that these lands obeyed their orders and paid them taxes. To achieve this, they had to behave like Italian princes, to decide which rulers were their friends and which their enemies, to have an army and sometimes to go to war. In this way they were quite unlike modern popes whom the world expects to be men of peace above all else.

22 The Papal States in the late fifteenth century.

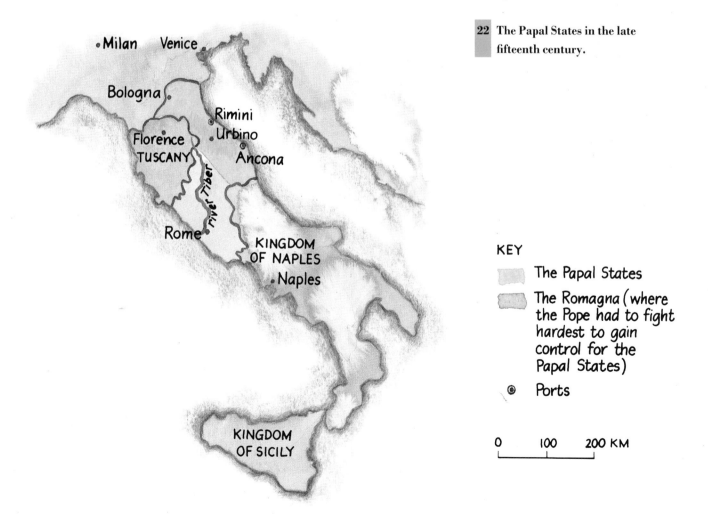

KEY

The Papal States

The Romagna (where the Pope had to fight hardest to gain control for the Papal States)

◉ Ports

0   100   200 KM

24 Platina, a famous humanist, being appointed by Pope Sixtus IV to take charge of the Vatican Library. By Melozzo da Forli (1438–94).

In the hundred years after 1417, though they failed as religious leaders (see Chapter 4), the popes succeeded as Italian princes. They brought the Papal States firmly under control. They increased their income by raising taxes, and made Rome once again the centre of the government of the Church. The population of the city tripled, reaching 100,000 by 1510.

The popes as patrons

The popes were Renaissance princes. Many of them had had humanist teachers and, living in Rome, they loved the idea of reviving the greatness of its past. Pope Nicholas V (1447–55) was a generous patron of the arts because he believed the Church would benefit. He said:

> **23** To create faith in the minds of the uneducated masses, there must be something which appeals to the eye . . . Noble buildings . . . would greatly improve the reputation of the popes.
>
> Pope Nicholas V, speech on his deathbed, 1455

Look at sources 25 and 26.
1 Describe briefly what each picture shows.
2 Which of these adjectives in your opinion goes best with each picture: light, cheerful, serious, colourful, monumental, delightful, grand, impressive.
3 From your study of the two pictures, what do you think are the main differences between Early and High Renaissance styles?

The High Renaissance in Rome

As the popes grew more powerful and richer, they were able to make themselves the best patrons of artists in Italy. They persuaded some of the finest architects, painters, sculptors and writers to come to Rome which by 1490 took over from Florence as the leading artistic centre of Europe.

At the same time a change took place in the artists' style. Art historians describe the Florence of the Medicis as the Early Renaissance and the later

25 Botticelli's *Primavera*, painted in Florence in about 1482.

26 Raphael's *School of Athens*, painted in Rome in 1510–11.

post-1490 Roman period the High Renaissance. Source 25 is an example of the Early Renaissance style, while source 26 is from the High Renaissance period.

Julius II: warrior pope and Renaissance patron

The tall figure standing in the centre of source 24 is Cardinal Giuliano della Rovere. He became Pope Julius II in 1503. He was sixty, short-tempered and strong-willed. He enjoyed wearing armour and led his troops to war against cities in the Papal States. He conquered Perugia and brought the Marches under control (see the map on page 43). He organised the League of Cambrai which defeated Venice in 1509. When asked how a statue of him should look, he said: 'Put a sword in my hand, not a book.'

Pope Julius was also a patron on a grand scale, giving important work to three of the finest artists of the High Renaissance: Michelangelo, sculptor and painter; Bramante, architect; and Raphael, painter.

He employed Michelangelo (see pages 69–73) first to carve for him a colossal tomb and then to paint the ceiling of the Sistine Chapel in the Vatican Palace. Michelangelo was as strong-willed as Julius was and they had furious rows. On one occasion, when the artist refused to work as fast as the Pope wanted, Julius threatened to have him thrown off the scaffolding.

Julius employed Bramante (1444–1514) as his architect and together they planned vast additions to the Vatican Palace and also a new Basilica of St Peter's (see Chapter 6). Bramante did his best work in Rome including a small round church, usually known as the 'Tempietto' or 'little temple', which influenced the work of many later architects.

Raphael (1483–1520), a distant relation of Bramante, had already amazed Florence by the skill, charm and speed of his painting. He, too, came to Rome and, even though he was still in his twenties, Julius gave him a free hand to decorate some of the large official rooms in the Vatican Palace. The paintings and designs which resulted (see source 29) were among Raphael's finest works.

27 *The Creation of Man* **painted by Michelangelo on the ceiling of the Sistine Chapel.**

28 Bramante's Tempietto, finished
after 1511.

29 Raphael: *Miraculous Draught of
Fishes.*

Review and Assessment

In what ways did Rome become more important between 1400 and 1513?

30 A view of Rome in 1493.

1 Study source 30.
  a What are the buildings in the top right of the picture under the words 'palatium papae'?
  b How had Rome changed as a city since 1400

2 Re-read pages 42–44.
In 1400, Rome was much less important in Italy and in Europe than Florence, Milan and Venice. Below is a list of possible causes for Rome's lack of importance at the beginning of the fifteenth century. Choose from the list those causes which you know to be true and write them down.

A Rome was not on any important trade-routes.

B There were no good artists in Italy in 1400.

C There were two quarrelling popes, one at Avignon in France, the other in Rome.

D Rome was a dangerous place to live because of the fighting between its leading families.

E The popes were very religious and did not want wealth or power.

3 Look back to pages 43–44.
 a What were the Papal States?
 b Show why they were important to the popes of the fifteenth century (i) for economic reasons, and (ii) for political reasons.

4 A modern historian, Giovanni Procacci, sums up the career of Julius II like this:

> **31** Julius II . . . completed the work of extending the central Italian lands under papal rule . . . and strengthened the finances of the papal state . . . In 1525 the taxes [paid to the pope] were double what they had been in 1492 and this made it possible for him to continue the great public works begun by the late fifteenth-century popes.
>
> G. Procacci, *History of the Italian People*, 1968

Study source 31 and read pages 45–47
 a Explain why Pope Julius spent so much time at war.
 b He was proud to think of himself as the warrior-pope, with a sword rather than a book in his hand. How successful was he in making himself and the popes who came after him more powerful?
 c How did the popes raise the money for their 'great public works'?

5 **a** When did Rome take over from Florence as the artistic centre of Italy?
 b What artists did Julius II employ and what changes did they make to the Vatican Palace and to other buildings in Rome?
 c How important were these changes in the history of European art?

6 Do you agree with the view that though the popes were successful as Italian princes between 1400 and 1513, this political success harmed them as leaders of the Christian Church in western and central Europe? Explain your answer.

4 Society in fifteenth-century Italy

The Renaissance brought swift and obvious changes to the art and architecture of Italy. It also caused changes in other aspects of life, but these changes took longer to happen and were much less obvious.

Religion

In 1400 virtually everyone in Europe believed in God and thought of themselves as Christians. Religion affected their daily lives much more directly than it does the lives of most Europeans nowadays. For example, Francesco Datini, a wealthy merchant from Prato near Florence, noted in his diary for August 1399 how, with 30,000 others, he joined a pilgrimage. The aim of this pilgrimage was to persuade God to prevent the plague from coming to Florence:

> **1** For nine days that the pilgrimage lasted, we walked barefoot . . . none of us might eat any meat, nor take off his white clothes, nor lie in bed.
>
> Quoted by Iris Origo, *The Merchant of Prato*, 1957

His wife, Margherita Datini, wrote to her husband about Fra (Brother) Giovanni, a Dominican friar:

> **2** You will do well to hasten as much as you can, for never has this friar preached better sermons than now . . .
>
> Quoted by Iris Origo, *The Merchant of Prato*, 1957

1 **What would you think today of a rich merchant who behaved like Datini in 1399?**
2 **What do sources 1 and 2 tell you about the religious beliefs of the Datinis?**

Francesco Datini followed his wife's advice and was so impressed by Brother Giovanni's sermons that he changed his will and left most of his fortune to the poor.

Most Italians were like the Datinis. The Christian religion was part and parcel of their lives. They believed the Bible to be the Word of God and attended the church service of Mass at least a few times each year. If they led bad lives they expected to go to Hell where they would stay in everlasting pain. If they were good they would go to Heaven and to a wonderful, also everlasting, life.

3 Source 3 was seen every day by people praying in Santa Maria Novella. What did it tell them about the Christian Church?

The Church

Source 3 is a fresco painting in the church of Santa Maria Novella in Florence. Its aim is to make clear the power of the Christian Church.

3 *The Triumph of the Church.* This fresco was painted in 1367 by Andrea da Firenze.

The clergy, that is priests, friars, monks and nuns, made up about 2% of the population. They explained what was good and what evil. Disagreeing with the Church was dangerous. It was called heresy and you could be put to death for heresy by burning at the stake. Quarrelling with church leaders was also dangerous as it could lead to excommunication. If you were excommunicated, you could not attend mass nor could you have a Christian burial. If a town or country misbehaved, a pope could, by an 'interdict', forbid priests to hold mass or burials. Pope Alexander VI threatened Florence with an interdict when it supported Savonarola in his demands that the Church should be reformed (see page 53).

There were church buildings everywhere. Homes and streets would be decorated with crosses and with pictures of the Virgin Mary.

However, all was not well with the Christian Church. The popes won back political power in Italy, but their reputation in Europe as church leaders got worse. They seemed interested only in Italian politics, in spending money and in looking after their relatives and illegitimate children.

Much of this poor reputation was deserved. For example, Alexander VI (1492–1503) was first a politician, then a priest. He had many lovers and children. The commander of his army was one of his sons, Cesare Borgia (see page 74), who almost certainly murdered his elder brother and brother-in-law. Alexander sold off top church jobs to the highest bidder or gave them to his relatives. He threw huge parties and encouraged his cardinals (his senior councillors) to do the same. Cardinal Cornaro once gave a meal of sixty-five courses, all served on plates of the finest silver.

Source 4 is part of a pamphlet published in Rome in 1501 while Rodrigo Borgia (Pope Alexander VI) was still alive. It read:

> **4** There is no sort of wickedness which is not practised in the palace of the pope . . . Rodrigo Borgia could not be more evil. He overturns all justice, human and divine.

Quoted by J.R. Hale, *Renaissance Europe 1480–1520*, 1971

Giovanni de' Medici, son of Lorenzo the Magnificent, became a cardinal at the age of fourteen thanks to his father's influence. He became Pope Leo X in 1513 when he was thirty-eight. He too looked after his relatives and was also a great spender. The saying went in Rome: 'He [Leo X] could no more save a thousand ducats than a stone could fly.' He enjoyed hunting, gambling and holding enormous parties with joke dishes like pies out of which nightingales flew!

Though many of the clergy led pious lives, did good works and were respected by their local communities, there was also much slackness in the Church. There were too many bishops absent from their dioceses and too many poorly-educated priests. The Franciscan and Dominican orders of friars,

5 Pope Leo X (1513–21), painted by Raphael. With him are two cardinals, Giulio de' Medici and Luigi de Rossi.

which had been founded in the thirteenth century to spread the Word of God, spent too much time squabbling with each other. Monks and nuns who were supposed to be devoting their lives entirely to the worship of God, cut off from the opposite sex, often took lovers.

More and more people came to believe that the Church needed to improve itself, to reform. But most of the demands for reform came from elsewhere, particularly from Europe north of the Alps rather than from Italy. John Colet, preaching in London in 1513, spoke for reformers all over Europe when he said:

> **6** The Church has become a machine for taking money from the poor instead of handing down Christ's teaching to them in love.
>
> Quoted by J.R. Hale, *Renaissance Europe 1480–1520*, 1971

Humanism and religious belief

Though virtually everyone in the fifteenth century thought of themselves as Christian, the humanism of the Renaissance made educated people more interested in the life now on earth than the life to come after death. It also made them prouder of human achievements. They were more ready to question and to criticise the teachings of the past, including those of the Church. Though most Europeans took Christian teachings and church attendance seriously until the end of the nineteenth century, the Renaissance began to loosen the firm hold on people's beliefs which religion had previously held, and in particular to lessen the influence of the priests and leaders of the church.

The tragedy of Savonarola

The extraordinary life and death of Fra Girolamo Savonarola (1452–98) showed how violent and angry people could become about religious matters, and how closely religion was linked to politics.

Savonarola was born in Ferrara in 1452. He joined the Dominican order of friars and came to Florence at the age of twenty-nine. His home was the Convent of San Marco, of which he became Prior (head). He was a small, thin, ugly man with a large, hooked nose and flashing eyes. He preached electrifying sermons which attracted so many people that he had to move from San Marco to the cathedral to deliver them.

Savonarola was a reformer. He thought that the Church was in a terrible state and that most people, priests as well as ordinary folk, cared too much about themselves and their possessions. Most princes (including Lorenzo de' Medici) were tyrants, misruled their subjects and forgot the laws of God.

What was unusual about Savonarola was that he claimed to be a prophet and to be able to see the future through the help of God. Unless the Florentines

1 Look back to pages 42–44.

1 Look back to pages 42–44.
  a) Of which saint did the popes believe themselves to be the successors?
  b) Why was Rome the capital city of Christianity?
2 What powers did the Church have against individuals and groups who disobeyed it? Why did these powers frighten ordinary people?
3 What did the popes do which lowered people's opinion of them?

7 Savonarola, painted by Bartolommeo della Porta (1427–1517).

1 What were the main reasons for Savonarola gaining the support of the people of Florence?

changed their ways, he warned, the most dreadful things would happen to them. In a sermon to a packed cathedral in 1492, Savonarola demanded:

> **8** Repent [show that you are sorry], O Florence, while there is still time . . . Clothe thyself in the white garments of purification. Wait no longer, for there is no further time for repentance.
>
> Quoted by C. Hibbert, *The Rise and Fall of the House of Medici*, 1974

In a series of terrifying sermons he told the congregation how he saw the Sword of the Lord hanging in a darkened sky over the city and foretold plague, war, tempests and floods. These prophecies seemed to come true. Lorenzo de' Medici suddenly died in 1492. In 1494 a huge French army marched into Italy. Savonarola welcomed the French as 'the arm of the Lord', the Medici family fled from the city and, as the French marched south, Savonarola became leader of a new republic which aimed to make the Florentines obey the laws of God. An informant of the Duke of Mantua reported in 1494:

> **9** . . . a Dominican friar has so terrified all the Florentines that three days in the week they fast on bread and water . . . All the girls and many of the wives have taken refuge in convents so that only men and youths and old women are seen on the street.
>
> Quoted by C. Hibbert, *The Rise and Fall of the House of Medici*, 1974

Bands of children went round the city looking for make-up, mirrors, expensive clothes, chessboards, dice, pictures and drawings. They looked for anything in fact which might distract citizens from a simple life devoted to God's service. Luca Landucci, who had a chemist's shop, was delighted that:

> **10** . . . his children were in Savonarola's blessed bands and were thought so highly of that everyone avoided bad behaviour.
>
> L. Landucci, *A Florentine Diary*, 1450–1516

2 Who were 'the blessed bands' of children in 1494 to whom Landucci (source 10) refers? Why did their actions please Landucci and many other Florentines?

However, Savonarola had powerful enemies both inside and outside Florence. The most dangerous outside the city was Pope Alexander VI who hated him both for his friendship with the French and for his demands that the Church be reformed. Inside the city, the Compagnacci, a group of rich young nobles, refused to accept the changes he ordered. They banged drums at his sermons and paid boys to throw stones at his supporters.

In 1498 the city turned against him:

> **11** Savonarola's supporters were losing ground [in 1497] . . . There had been poor harvests . . . starving people had fallen down and died in the streets; there had been an outbreak of plague. Savonarola's hero, King

Charles of France, had not returned Pisa to Florence as he had promised . . .

C. Hibbert, *The Rise and Fall of the House of Medici*, 1974

The French left Italy and the Pope threatened Florence with an interdict. Savonarola's prophecies were not coming true anymore. In the spring of that year, the Franciscan friars, bitter rivals to the Dominicans, challenged him to ordeal by fire. If God really spoke through him, they taunted, fire would not harm him and his supporters.

On 7 April 1498 two lines, about thirty metres long, of sticks soaked in oil were laid out in the Piazza della Signoria, the main square of Florence. It had been agreed that they would be lit and in the fiery space between them would walk Fra Giuliano for the Franciscans and Fra Domenico representing Savonarola and the Dominicans. Savonarola had agreed that he would leave Florence for ever if Fra Domenico was burnt.

The friars arrived and the Franciscans were quickly ready for the ordeal to begin. The Dominicans, however, found excuse after excuse to delay until a heavy thunderstorm brought things to an end for the day.

This was too much for the Florentines. They rioted against Savonarola who was arrested, found guilty of heresy and, with two companions, burnt to death. As the flames surrounded him, a jeer from the crowd was heard. 'O prophet, now is the time for a miracle! Prophet, save yourself.'

3 List the reasons given in source 11 for the drop in Savonarola's support. Which were economic, which social and which political?

4 a) Describe what you can see in source 12.
   b) What event in 1498 turned the Florentines violently against Savonarola?
   c) For what offence was he brought to trial and found guilty?

12 The execution of Savonarola in the Piazza della Signoria in Florence. A fifteenth-century painting by an unknown artist.

Women in Renaissance Italy

Francesco Datini, the rich merchant of Prato, married his wife, Margherita, when he was forty-one and she was sixteen. He chose her because she was pretty, healthy and from a good family. He expected her to bear him plenty of children and be a good housewife. In fact they did not succeed in having any children of their own, though he fathered at least one child by a servant.

As far as the housekeeping was concerned, he never stopped giving his wife instructions. Here is a typical letter from 1401:

13 Tomorrow morning, send back the jar of dried raisins and the bread . . . Remember to wash the mule's feet with hot water down to her hoofs. And my hose [stockings] made and then soled . . . and give some millet that is left to you to the nag . . . and hasten the sale of the two barrels of wine.

Quoted by Iris Origo, *The Merchant of Prato*, 1957

Early in his marriage Francesco made his young wife furious by suggesting that one of her letters to him must have been written by someone else. It was too well-composed, he thought, 'to be by a young female.'

William Caxton (c.1422–91), who introduced printing into England, had much the same view of the role of women. He wrote:

14 The women of this country [England] should be wise, pleasant, humble, discreet, sober, chaste, obedient to their husbands, . . . ever busy and never idle, temperate [gentle] in speaking and virtuous in all their works . . .

Quoted by J.R. Hale, *Renaissance Europe*, 1480–1520

15 *Birth of the Virgin* in Santa Maria Novella, painted in 1490 by Domenico del Ghirlandaio (1449–94). Ghirlandaio sets the religious story in a fashionable Florentine merchant's home. The young lady standing with her four attendants is Lucrezia Tornabuoni, daughter of Giovanni Tornabuoni who was paying for this chapel's wall-paintings.

Datini and Caxton were typical of the fifteenth century. Most people at that time thought women were second-class citizens, whose lives should be given to their husbands, their families and to religion.

However, women from poorer families had to work. In Florence many were ribbonmakers, dressmakers and shopkeepers. Though they could join the craft guilds, they could not hold senior positions in them. Women had less education than men and no political rights.

The main aim of girls' parents was to make a good marriage for them and see them bear children. Women would be about twenty when they married, men would be in their thirties, and a high death-rate led to frequent re-marriage. Parents played a large part in choosing the marriage partners of their children. Love did not matter. Health, wealth and the reputation of the family did.

Cosimo de' Medici married Contessina de' Bardi, the daughter of one of his father's banking friends. They had children, but little else in common. Cosimo bought himself a pretty slave girl. Their son, Carlo, grew up in the Medici household and became a priest. Lorenzo de' Medici married Clarice Orsini when he was nineteen and she sixteen. His parents selected her because the Orsini were among the noblest of Roman families and her mother was sure that she would be good at bearing children. (She eventually produced ten.) Lorenzo and Clarice seem to have liked each other and she put up with his many well-known love affairs without fuss. However she had little time for his humanist friends and sacked Politian, one of the most famous, from the position of tutor to their children because he was not religious enough for her.

A few women became famous in their own right. For example, Isabella d'Este, Duchess of Mantua, built up one of the best collections of paintings in Italy; Caterina Sforza defended the town of Forli from an attack by papal troops under Cesare Borgia with great skill and courage; and Vittoria Colonna was highly thought of for her poetry. Such women were the exception.

16 Isabella d'Este. This charcoal sketch was done by Leonardo da Vinci as a study for a portrait that was never painted.

Science

As educated people began to ask questions about the world in which they lived and were less ready to be told the right answers by their religious leaders, scientific thinking became possible.

Modern scientists help us to a better understanding of the world and the universe by careful observation. They ask questions about the things which they observe and suggest explanations for them. They then carry out experiments to test the accuracy of their explanations. Scientists are curious and do not accept explanations, however widely believed by others, if they do not fit the facts. Take, for example, the movements of the earth and the sun. Everyone in Europe in 1500 believed that the sun revolved round the earth.

However a Polish thinker, Copernicus, found that his observations of the sun and planets would only make sense if the earth revolved round the sun. He published his ideas in 1543. Later, in the early seventeenth century, Kepler in Germany and Galileo in Italy proved Copernicus' ideas to be true. Church leaders could not believe such ideas could be true. They declared Galileo to be guilty of heresy and forbade him to teach for the rest of his life!

The beginnings of modern scientific thinking date from the sixteenth and seventeenth centuries. Earlier, in Renaissance Italy, hardly anyone thought scientifically. Most people believed in magic. Princes kept astrologers at their courts to study the movement of the stars which they thought controlled human events. Some men, known as alchemists, also believed that by a magic method they could change cheap metals into gold. However, the experiments of alchemists did increase knowledge about different metals. For example, Paracelsus (c.1490–1541), an extraordinary Swiss alchemist, was interested in how metals like mercury and sulphur could be used in medicine. Slowly chemistry began to emerge from alchemy.

Leonardo da Vinci

Was Leonardo a scientist?

Leonardo da Vinci was one of the few Renaissance figures who thought scientifically. As he grew older he became more and more interested in science, mathematics and technology, and less in painting.

We have seen how Leonardo began his career in Florence and then moved to Milan. From Milan he returned to Florence in 1500 and lived there until 1506. He was by then fifty-three and spent the last years of his life in Milan again, then in Rome working for Giovanni de' Medici (the future Pope Leo X), and finally in France at the invitation of Francis I. He died in France in 1519.

Most of his scientific work is in his notebooks which show that he was always asking questions about human beings and the world in which they lived. He observed closely and drew not only beautifully but with great accuracy (see source 19). As Leonardo walked in the mountains he found the fossils of sea-shells. The mountains, he noted correctly, must once have lain below an ancient sea. Watching the flight of birds made him think about the nature of flight and to try, without success, to design a flying machine.

His notebooks are full of remarkable technological ideas, none of which came to very much in reality. He designed cannon, a huge crossbow, machines for defending fortifications and mechanical gears. He also produced numerous plans for draining marshes and an ambitious scheme, which he persuaded the government of Florence to take seriously for a few months, of diverting the

17 A drawing of a war machine by Leonardo. This is a chariot armed with scythes. The writing is in Leonardo's mirror-handwriting.

River Arno in a huge canal round Pisa so ships could sail directly into Florence. It was a colossal project which would have been difficult and expensive even with modern earth-moving machinery.

Leonardo was very interested in anatomy (the study of the human body). Paolo Giovio, doctor of Pope Leo X, who came from near Milan and was a teenager when Leonardo was working there described how:

18 In order that he might be able to paint the various joints and muscles as they bend and stretch according to the laws of nature, he dissected [cut up] the corpses of criminals, not bothered by this inhuman and nauseating [sickening] work. He then listed with extreme accuracy all the different parts, down to the smallest veins.

P. Giovio, *In Praise of Leonardo da Vinci*, 1527

His interest in anatomy started from his need as a painter to show the human body as realistically as possible, but he pursued his anatomical studies far beyond his artistic needs. He dissected animals as well as humans and drew exactly what he found. The heart particularly interested him and he seems to have got close to discovering how blood circulates through the body, a discovery which was eventually made more than a century later by Sir William Harvey.

Leonardo's problem was that he was ahead of his time. He lived among and worked for people who thought of him mainly as an artist. His scientific ideas were written in his mirror-writing in his private notebooks and never published. The life of the man who did the most to put anatomy onto a scientific basis was quite different. Andreas Vesalius (1514–64), who was born in Brussels and taught at the University of Padua, spent all his life studying anatomy and had his discoveries printed and published in a book called the *Fabric of the Human Body* which quickly became famous all over Europe.

Did Leonardo have too many talents for his own good?

During his lifetime, people realised that his scientific and technical interests were unusual for an artist. An unknown Florentine wrote in 1518:

19 A drawing of hearts and blood vessels by Leonardo.

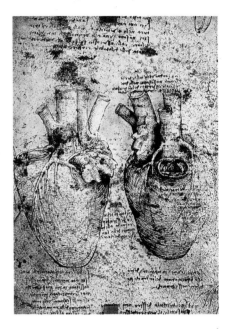

1 **What evidence have you that Leonardo, in drawing and painting, was one of the best artists of the Renaissance?**

2 **Why are sources 20, 23 and 24 useful for trying to find out why Leonardo completed so few paintings?**

3 **Compare sources 20 and 23 on Leonardo. How are they different? Which judgement do you prefer and why?**

4 **Using sources 20–24, write a paragraph explaining why Leonardo, in comparison with other artists who lived as long as he, finished so little.**

5 **Which sources did you find backed each other up as you answered question 4? Which ones were in conflict with the others?**

22 *Mona Lisa*, **painted by Leonardo in about 1503.**

20 Greatly talented in mathematics, he was no less so in the science of perspective, while in sculpture and design he far surpassed all others. He made many excellent inventions but because it was hard for him to be satisfied with his work we find but few paintings from his hand.

Anonymous book in the National Library Florence, from about 1518

No-one can doubt Leonardo's astonishing talents as a painter. The *Mona Lisa* (source 22) in the Louvre, Paris, is the world's most famous painting. In his lifetime he already had a very high reputation, as Vasari wrote:

21 He drew on paper so carefully and well that no-one has ever equalled him . . . The *Mona Lisa* is an extraordinary example of how art can imitate Nature . . . it was painted in a manner to cause the boldest artists to despair.

Vasari, *Lives*, 1550

But other writers note how few paintings he finished. Kenneth Clark, biographer of Leonardo, wrote in 1939:

23 His innumerable drawings of mathematical games . . . leave us lamenting the waste of Leonardo's time . . . These figures have as much to do with geometry as a crossword puzzle has to do with literature.

K. Clark, *Leonardo da Vinci*, 1939

Vasari comments on how Leonardo passed his time in Rome:

24 On the back of a strange lizard he fixed with a mixture of quicksilver wings which quivered as it walked; and having given it eyes, horns and a beard, taming it and keeping it in a box, he made all his friends to whom he showed it fly with fear . . . He had many such foolish tricks.

Vasari, *Lives*, 1550

Technology

The three major technological advances of the fifteenth century were printing, ocean navigation and artillery. All three were discovered outside Italy, but quickly affected the Italians, for both good and ill.

Printing

Johann Gutenberg produced the first printed books in Europe in the German metal-working town of Mainz in the 1440s, though the Chinese and Japanese had discovered printing centuries earlier. The vital invention in Europe was movable type made of an alloy of tin, lead and antimony (a silvery-white metal). Such type was easy to shape and gave a crisp appearance to each letter on the printed page. A good example of Gutenberg's work is the Bible of 1456.

Printing then spread rapidly across Europe. Italy's most famous printer/publisher was Aldus Manutius of Venice. He printed many Latin and Greek editions which were much the same size as modern paperbacks. By 1500 236 towns in Europe had their own printers who, by then, had printed at least 10 million books under 40,000 different titles.

It is hard to exaggerate the importance of printing. Because books became cheaper, more people read them. Travellers carried them easily from one part of Europe to another and new ideas spread more quickly.

Ocean navigation

During the fifteenth century Portuguese and Spanish sailors struck more confidently away from land into the vastness of the Atlantic Ocean. They were able to do so because of their technologically advanced 'caravel' ships with more sails and a fixed rudder, and because they had found out how to fix their position out of sight of land by mathematical calculations based on the position of the sun and stars. For such calculations they used instruments like the astrolabe, which gave the position of the sun and stars for each day of the year.

Christopher Columbus (an Italian working for the Spanish) reached America in 1492 and Vasco de Gama, working for the Portuguese, reached India in 1498. The new sea-routes from Europe round Africa to the East and westwards to the new continent of America brought greater trade and wealth to the countries of Western Europe, particularly to the Portuguese, Spanish, Dutch, English and French. The age when Italian cities stood at the centre of Europe's trade came to an end. To add insult to injury, French and English ships entered the Mediterranean to compete there for trade as well.

Artillery

The explosive power of gunpowder (a mixture of sulphur, potassium nitrate and charcoal) had been discovered in Europe in the thirteenth century, about four centuries later than in China. During the fifteenth century the French had the best artillery, bronze cannons on wheeled carriages which horses pulled at the speed of a marching army. These cannons helped the French win many victories in Italy between 1494 and 1515 (see Chapter 5). However, in 1525 a Spanish army armed with the arquebus or handgun defeated the French at Pavia. The Spanish commander surprised the French on open ground and his hand-gunners mowed down first the French cavalry, then the infantry.

Again, no good came to Italy from this technological advance. Artillery helped first the French, then the Spanish conquer most of the Italian peninsula. You will find more about this in Chapter 5.

25 The Gutenberg Bible.

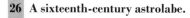

6 **Link these jumbled words correctly by taking one from each of (i), (ii), and (iii):**
a **(i) Copernicus; Gutenberg; Aldus Manutius. (ii) publisher; scientist; printer. (iii) Venice; Mainz; Poland.**
b **(i) printing; navigation; artillery. (ii) Spanish; stars; metal alloy. (iii) movable type; arquebus; astrolabe.**
7 **Which nations made the best use of the technological advances in navigation and in artillery? How did these advances affect Italy?**

26 A sixteenth-century astrolabe.

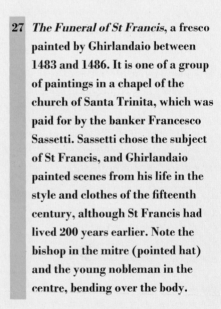

Review and Assessment

Continuity and change in fifteenth-century Italy

Historians are interested in the Italian Renaissance because of the important changes it brought to the ways in which Europeans thought and acted. Naturally these changes get most of the attention in history books. However if you had lived in fifteenth-century Italy, many aspects of your life would not have changed at all. This was particularly so if you were one of that vast majority of people who lived off the land and could not read or write. For such people the continuities of existence (that is the similarities of your life compared to those of your grandparents and your grandchildren) were much more obvious than the changes.

27 *The Funeral of St Francis*, a fresco painted by Ghirlandaio between 1483 and 1486. It is one of a group of paintings in a chapel of the church of Santa Trinita, which was paid for by the banker Francesco Sassetti. Sassetti chose the subject of St Francis, and Ghirlandaio painted scenes from his life in the style and clothes of the fifteenth century, although St Francis had lived 200 years earlier. Note the bishop in the mitre (pointed hat) and the young nobleman in the centre, bending over the body.

1 What do the following tell you about the importance of the Church in the everyday life of the fifteenth century:
a the Sassetti Chapel;
b the way Ghirlandaio decorated the chapel;
c the fact that almost all Ghirlandaio's paintings are religious ones?

2 Who was the most popular preacher in Florence in 1490? Do you think the city was more or less religous in 1490 than in 1400, or much the same?

3 Vespasiano de' Bisticci, a Florentine bookseller, had this opinion of women. He wrote in the 1470s:

28 Women should follow these rules: the first is that they should bring up their children in the fear of God; and the second is that they should keep quiet in church, and I would add, stop talking in other places as well, for they cause much mischief thereby.

V. de' Bisticci, *Vite* (Lives), about 1475

a What in Bisticci's opinion was the main task of women and what was their main failing?

b Compare source 28 with the opinions of Datini and Caxton (see page 56). How is it similar; how different?

4 Study Ghirlandaio's picture of the *Birth of the Virgin* (see page 56).

a There are eleven women in the picture. One, St Anne who was the mother of the baby Virgin Mary, lies on the bed. What are the other ten doing?

b What does the picture tell you about women in fifteenth-century Florence?

5

29 Printing was important because it helped to diffuse [spread] Renaissance ideas by making books much cheaper and more easily available. The printing press in Florence produced 1,025 copies of Plato's *Dialogues* in 1485–6 in the time a scribe would have taken to produce a single copy . . . [However] even in Florence the demand for classics was very limited compared to vernacular romances [love stories written in Italian] and religious writing.

Alison Brown, *The Renaissance*, 1988

What according to source 29 changed greatly as a result of the invention of printing, and what changed very little?

6 Whose way of life changed most and whose least between 1400 and 1500; that of a merchant's wife, of a parish priest, of a soldier or of a book-seller? Explain your choices.

5 The end of the Italian Renaissance

An 'age of calamities'

One of Italy's earliest and greatest historians was Francesco Guicciardini (1483–1540). In his opinion the time when Lorenzo de' Medici was master of Florence was a golden age for the whole of Italy. Guicciardini's *History of Italy* which begins in 1492 (the date of Lorenzo's death) and finishes in 1534 starts with a glowing description of Italy during Lorenzo's lifetime:

> **1** Who does not know what Italy is? A province, queen of all others because of . . . the great number and skill of men ready for all sorts of work and projects, the amount of things useful to mankind, the greatness and beauty of so many cities, the home of religion and the ancient glory of Empire.
>
> Guicciardini, *History of Italy*, 1561

In Guicciardini's opinion, Lorenzo's death in 1492 was followed by an 'age of calamities' which reached its lowest point in 1527 when an army, acting in the name of the Emperor Charles V, did terrible things to the city of Rome during the so-called 'Sack of Rome' (see page 67). By then foreign rulers controlled much of Italy.

The French invasions

This age of calamities began with the invasion of Italy by the French in 1494. By this time France was among the most powerful states in Europe. Its kings had won control over its previously over-mighty nobles and had also got the upper hand in its centuries-old rivalry with England. It had a large and well-trained army and its new king, Charles VIII, wanted to win glory by military success.

His chance came in 1494 when the king of Naples died. Charles believed that through his relatives he had a fair claim to the vacant throne of Naples. He therefore led his army into Italy to make good that claim. The size, discipline and guns of the French army amazed the Italians who offered little resistance. Guicciardini records how terrifyingly different the French army seemed:

> **2** They would face the enemy like a wall without ever breaking rank . . . their great amount of artillery of a sort never before seen in Italy made ridiculous all old methods of attack . . . Their cannon, drawn not by oxen as was the custom in Italy, but by horses . . . were led right up to the walls and set in position with unbelievable speed . . . They used this devilish weapon not only in besieging cities but on the battlefield.

Guicciardini, *History of Italy*, 1561

Charles swept into Naples and had himself crowned king. That, however, was the end of his success. Most Italian states, supported by Spain and the German Emperor, united together against Charles who had great difficulty in fighting his way home.

Though Charles died in 1498, the kings of France now had a taste for Italian adventures. Louis XII fought in Italy off-and-on for thirteen years (1499–1512). He drove Lodovico Sforza, Leonardo's patron, from Milan in 1502, divided the kingdom of Naples with the Spanish, and heavily defeated the proud republic of Venice at Agnadello in 1509. However the Italian states, led by Pope Julius II and supported by the king of Spain and the German Emperor, united once again and drove Louis XII back to France in 1512.

The French returned in 1515, this time led by Louis' successor, Francis I, another young man thirsty for glory. He won back the Duchy of Milan by a famous victory at Marignano in 1515 but was spectacularly defeated at Pavia in 1525 by a combined army of Spanish and Germans fighting for the Emperor Charles V. Francis was captured at Pavia and taken to Spain as a prisoner.

Pavia was a decisive battle in European history. It meant that the Habsburg family, which, in the person of the Emperor Charles V united Spain, Austria and parts of Germany, would be in charge of Italy, not the Valois family of France.

1 Why did Charles VIII invade Italy?

2 In Guicciardini's opinion, why was the French army so difficult to defeat?

3 How successful was Charles' invasion a) in the short-run, and b) in the long run?

4 For what reasons does Guicciardini think that 1492 was a turning-point in the history of Italy?

3 Italy in the time of the French invasions 1494–1530.

FRANCE

Milan

Agnadello

Marignano

Pavia

Venice

Bologna

Pisa

Florence

OTTOMAN TURKS

PAPAL STATES

ADRIATIC SEA

Rome

CORSICA

Naples

KINGDOM OF NAPLES

SARDINIA

KEY

—— Charles VIII (outward)

—+— Charles VIII (homeward)

✗ Major battles

—— River

0   100   200 KM

KINGDOM OF SICILY

MEDITERRANEAN SEA

4 The Battle of Pavia. A German painting of around 1525.

The Sack of Rome, 1527

The pope of the time was a Medici, Clement VII, nephew of Lorenzo the Magnificent. He made the mistake of siding with the French and, in 1527, found himself cornered in Rome by a large German army sent against him by the Emperor Charles V. When that army reached Rome, it was in a very ugly mood. It had lost two commanders within a few weeks. Its discipline was poor and it had not been paid. It easily overcame the small garrison defending the walls of Rome and forced the pope and his cardinals to take refuge in the fortress of Sant' Angelo. (One cardinal had to be hauled to safety in a basket.)

The foreign soldiers then laid waste the city. They stripped priests naked, raped nuns and vandalised churches. The rich were held to ransom or tortured until they handed over their treasures. Many poor people were simply killed. As many as 8,000 may have died on the first day after the city fell.

This 'Sack of Rome', as it became known, was shocking by any standards, but it seemed particularly shocking since Rome was the capital of the Christian Church. Many Christians thought that these terrible events showed how angry God was with the state of the Church and with the evil ways of the popes.

The siege of Florence, 1529

The news from Rome caused Florence to revolt against the Medici. Remembering how Savonarola had driven out the Medici in 1494 and set up a religious republic, they again drove out the Medici and their friends, proclaimed a republic in the name of Christ and hoped that the French would come to their aid. Their hopes were in vain. Pope Clement VII, head of the Medici family, made his peace with the Emperor Charles V who, in return, sent his army to restore the Medici family to Florence.

40,000 Spanish troops laid siege to Florence in 1529. Behind fortifications designed by Michelangelo, one of the most famous artists of the Renaissance, the citizens held out bravely, though Michelangelo himself lost his nerve and fled. The city held out for ten months until August 1530. Only when it became clear that no help would come from France did the city finally surrender.

On their return, the Medici family had the leaders of this last Florentine republic tortured and executed. They forced the citizens to pay a huge fine. When Guicciardini returned to the city soon after the end of the siege, he found:

> 5 the people and their resources exhausted, all the houses around the city destroyed for miles and the peasants [from the surrounding countryside] . . . disappeared almost entirely . . .
>
> Guicciardini, *Ricordi* [*Memories*], 1576

To rule this most brilliant of the cities of the Italian Renaissance came Alessandro de' Medici, a dreadful young man who was eventually murdered by his equally dreadful cousin. Supported by the Habsburgs, the Medici family was to rule Florence for another two centuries.

6 *The Siege of Florence*, **by Vasari.**

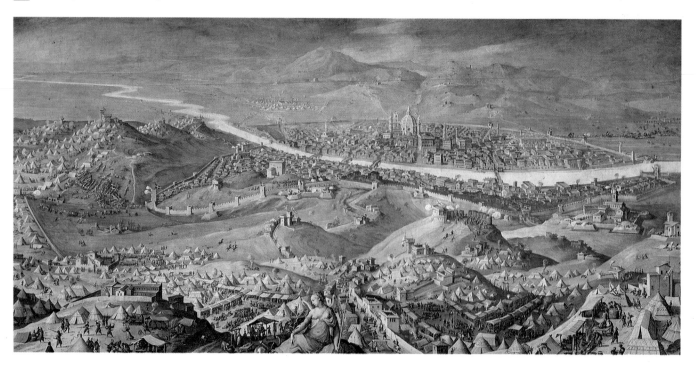

The end of the Renaissance in Italy

The Sack of Rome (1527) and the siege of Florence (1529–30) were disasters which in many ways marked the end of the Renaissance in Italy. Plagues added to the misery of the people. As goods were traded in ever-increasing amounts along the new sea-routes to India and America, northern Italy ceased to be the centre of European trade. The rich merchants who had given such encouragement to artists became fewer in number and, apart from in Venice, the number of outstanding painters, sculptors and architects dropped remarkably.

The cheerful confidence about the future which had been so much a part of the Renaissance evaporated in the miseries of 'the age of calamities'.

However, it would be wrong to think of the Renaissance coming to a sudden end. The Renaissance was made up of what people thought and artists' styles and methods. These changed slowly as one generation gave way to the next. In fact one of the greatest if not the greatest of the Renaissance artists, Michelangelo, lived for thirty-seven years after the Sack of Rome and completed some of his most important work in these years. And Venetian art was as fine in the sixteenth century as in the fifteenth.

Michelangelo: the greatest artist of them all?

Michelangelo (1475–1564), who was born when Lorenzo de' Medici was at the height of his powers and outlived the other great artists of the Renaissance by many years, lived long enough for Vasari to know him personally. He is the hero of Vasari's *Lives* and gets much the longest chapter. As Vasari himself put it:

> 7 Now I had not written the life of any living master . . . save only Michelangelo . . . I count it among the greatest blessings that I was born when Michelangelo was alive . . . and that he was so much a friend . . . All the three arts [painting, sculpture and architecture] were so perfected in him, that it is not found that among persons ancient and modern, in all the many years that the sun has been spinning around the heavens, God has granted this to any other but Michelangelo.

Vasari, *Lives*, 1550

1 Put these dates on a time-line and the correct event against each one:
1494, 1509, 1515, 1525, 1527, 1529;
Battle of Pavia, Sack of Rome, Battle of Marignano, Invasion of Charles VIII, Siege of Florence, Battle of Agnadello.
2 List the reasons why the years 1494–1530 are described by many historians as an 'age of calamities' for Italy.
3 List the main consequences of the foreign invasions under the following headings: political, religious, social and artistic.
4 a) What changes would people in the cities of northern Italy have noticed between 1494 and 1530?
b) To what extent would they thought of them as changes for the better or for the worse?

8 *The Last Judgement*. Michelangelo painted this scene in the Sistine Chapel in the Vatican.

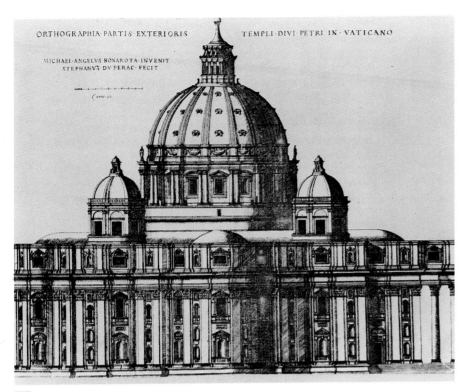

9 Michelangelo's design for the new St Peter's.

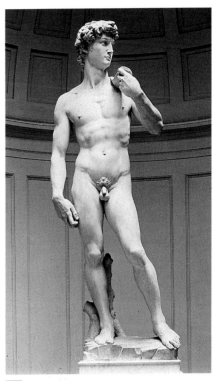

10 *David*. An example of Michelangelo's sculpture.

Read source 7 again.

1 Note down one fact which Vasari gives about Michelangelo (see pages 70–71) and one opinion.

2 What was Vasari's opinion of Michelangelo as an artist?

3 a) What were the main differences between Vasari's life of Michelangelo in comparison to his *Lives* of other artists?

b) How might these differences have influenced Vasari's opinions about Michelangelo?

c) Do they make Vasari's comments more reliable?

4 How might the circumstances which you have described in answer to question 3 have influenced Vasari's opinion of Michelangelo?

Michelangelo in Florence

Michelangelo was born near Florence in 1475. Sculpture was his first passion and his early carvings caught the eye of Lorenzo the Magnificent who took the talented youth into his household. Michelangelo made his reputation in Florence in 1504 when he completed a 14-foot (4.3 metres) high statue of David (source 10) which you can still see to this day in Florence. The original is now in a museum protected from the weather, but a copy stands in the Piazza della Signoria on the spot where the government of the city proudly placed the original after consulting the chief artists of the time.

Michelangelo in Rome

Pope Julius II then employed him in Rome both as a sculptor on his tomb and as a painter on the Sistine Chapel ceiling. After the death of Julius, Michelangelo worked sometimes in Florence, but mainly in Rome. In Florence he completed some powerful sculptures for the Medici family chapel in the church of San Lorenzo in 1524–34. In Rome he completed the huge and terrifying painting of the Last Judgement on the end wall of the Sistine Chapel in the years 1536–41 (see source 8).

However, the older he grew, the more time he spent as an architect. In the last years of his long life he had charge of the most important building project in Rome, the rebuilding of St Peter's (see source 9). The old basilica of St Peter's was more than 1,000 years old and falling down when Pope Julius II decided to rebuild it. He and later popes aimed to have the finest church in Europe built. They employed the best architects and were ready to spend a great deal of money on it.

11 The situation in 1544 as painted by Vasari. The large circular arches of Bramante's design, on which the dome would rest, are almost finished. Jutting out towards you is a low unfinished circular wall which Michelangelo had demolished soon after this picture was painted.

Michelangelo found this a frustrating task since money was short and progress slow. He undid much of the work of the previous architect, Antonio da Sangallo, because he thought it was too fussy. His aim was to get closer to the simpler and grander plans of Bramante. Though the famous front view of St Peter's (see page 5) is the work of later architects, the back (see source 12) is very much as Michelangelo planned it.

Unlike other leading artists of the time, Michelangelo preferred to work on his own. His energy and devotion to his work were remarkable. Though he became a rich man, he lived a simple life. There was a story that he usually wore his dogskin stockings so long that his skin came off with them when he got round to changing them. He seldom stopped working. Vasari tells how he slept little and would work through the night wearing a specially constructed cap which held a candle.

Michelangelo was deeply religious and a gifted poet as well as a painter, sculptor and architect. In his sculptures and paintings, especially the Sistine Chapel ceiling, he used the human body to express a wide range of ideas and feelings. Look again at the Creation of Man (page 46). God on the right is shown full of power, energy and movement. Through his outstretched finger He passes life into the laid-back figure of man who seems to have only just enough energy to reach out his hand. Michelangelo's influence on the next generation of painters was enormous.

12 The back of St Peter's today looks much as Michelangelo designed it – see source 9.

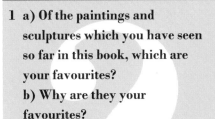

1 a) Of the paintings and sculptures which you have seen so far in this book, which are your favourites?
b) Why are they your favourites?

2 Do you have such a high opinion of Michelangelo as Vasari? If not, why not?

3 a) Draw a timeline of Michelangelo's life (1475 to 1564). Mark on it the dates of his most famous works: the statue of David (see page 71), the Sistine Chapel (page 46), the *Last Judgement* (page 70), the design of St Peter's (page 71).
Then add the dates of the death of Leonardo (see page 58), Raphael (page 46) and Bramante (page 46), the sack of Rome (page 67).
b) From this timeline, decide which ten years best mark the end of the Italian Renaissance: 1494–1504, 1510–1520, 1525–1535 or 1554–1564. Explain the thinking behind your choice.

Machiavelli: politician and political writer

Another eye-witness of the age of calamities, and a victim of them, was Niccolo Machiavelli (1469–1527), who was to become one of Europe's most famous writers about politics. He was born in Florence, the son of a lawyer. In 1498, when he was twenty-nine, he became a senior official of the Florentine government and travelled widely in Italy, France and Germany on government business. On these travels he met Cesare Borgia, the illegitimate son of Pope Alexander VI, who was then forcing much of central Italy to accept Borgia rule. Seeing the strength of the French army and Cesare Borgia's successful use of force, Machiavelli realised that Florence had no chance of staying free and independent unless it could greatly increase its military power. He tried without success to create an efficient army of Florentine citizens.

The Medici returned to Florence in 1512, overthrowing the government which had employed Machiavelli. He was sacked and for a short time imprisoned and tortured because he was suspected, wrongly, of plotting against the Medici. He spent the rest of his life on his farm outside the city trying to win the favour of the Medici so that he could resume his career in politics. In this he had little success, so he had the time to write the books on politics which made him famous.

Machiavelli was twenty-five when Charles VIII invaded Italy so he spent most of his adult life either dealing with or writing about the effects of the foreign invasions. In his books, the most important of which are *The Prince* and the *Discourses*, he compared events of his own time with those of ancient Greece and Rome, and tried to explain why some princes and city-states were successful and some were not. His particular hope was that an Italian prince might act on his advice and succeed in driving the foreigners from Italy. His most famous book, *The Prince*, was written in 1513 to persuade Lorenzo de' Medici (grandson of Lorenzo the Magnificent) to do just that. This is how *The Prince* ends:

> **13** See how Italy beseeches [begs] God to send someone to save her from those barbarous cruelties; see how eager and willing the country is to follow a banner, if only someone will raise it. And, at the present time it is impossible to see in what she can place more hope than in your illustrious House which with its fortune and prowess [skill] . . . can lead Italy to her salvation.

Machiavelli, *The Prince*, 1513

1 What is the 'illustrious House' in source 13? What did Machiavelli want it to do?

He died in 1527, deeply saddened by the events of his life. He looked back to what he thought of as the good old days of the proud, free, creative Florentine republic of the mid-fifteenth century when no foreign armies troubled Italy. Fortunately, he did not live long enough to see Spanish troops return the Medici to Florence in 1530.

Machiavelli's writings

What was new and to some people upsetting about Machiavelli's writings was that, instead of saying how rulers ought to rule, he described how rulers actually did rule and tried to work out how they were successful. This led him to the conclusion that if rulers were to look after their states properly, they might often have to act in apparently bad, unchristian ways; for example, lying, attacking enemies, terrifying people or even killing them. In his opinion:

14 A wise ruler cannot and should not keep his word if that would be to his disadvantage . . . If men were all good, this rule would not be good; but since men are a sorry lot and will not keep their promises, you likewise need not keep yours to them.

Machiavelli, *Discourses*, 1517

15 Machiavelli, painted in about 1515 by Santo di Tito.

He suggested that the cruel, lying and treacherous Cesare Borgia was a wise ruler. He wrote in *The Prince*:

16 I do not know of any better advice to give a new prince than the example of the deeds of Cesare Borgia ... [for example] Cesare Borgia was considered cruel; nonetheless his cruelty brought order to the Romagna [an Italian province], united it, restored it to peace and to obedience ... [Also] Cesare wanted to get rid of the Orsini family but he craftily hid his intentions so that the Orsini themselves made peace with him; ... The Duke [Cesare] got Paolo Orsini to think him a friend by many acts of kindness, giving him money, clothing, and horses so that the stupidity of the Orsini brought them to Sinigaglia [where Cesare had them murdered.]

Machiavelli, *The Prince*, 1513

To pretend that good people would naturally make good rulers was, in Machiavelli's opinion, foolish. Human beings behaved stupidly or badly more often than sensibly or well. Though most modern political writers would now agree with Machiavelli, many people, particularly church leaders in the sixteenth and seventeenth centuries, found his ideas shocking. It was not surprising that church leaders disliked his books since he wrote that the church was harming Italy:

17 Because of the bad example of the court [of the popes] of Rome, this land has lost all its devotion and religion; this in turn brings countless evils and disorders ... the Church has kept and still keeps our lands divided.

Machiavelli, *Discourses*, 1517

1 List the comments in sources 16 and 17 which a Christian would consider wrong.
2 Cesare Borgia was, by any standards, a bad man working for a corrupt family. How can Machiavelli argue his apparently evil actions like cruelty and cold-blooded murder were the actions of a sensible ruler?
3 What other comments of Machiavelli would church leaders not have liked?

Review and Assessment

The changing reputation of Machiavelli

1 The *Collins New Guild Dictionary* defines 'Machiavellian' as:

> **18** unscrupulous, crafty, one who practises the perfidious political doctrine of Machiavelli.

The entry for Niccolo Machiavelli in the *Encyclopaedia Britannica* (1973) is:

> **19** Italian statesman and writer, patriot and thinker of genius whose acute understanding of politics and profound insight into human nature produced masterpieces which have often been misjudged as immoral or cynical.

Explain the meaning of these words: perfidious, patriot, immoral, cynical.

2 List **a** four facts, and **b** two different points of view about Machiavelli.

3 In 1552 the Roman Catholic Church banned all Machiavelli's books, and after the St Bartholomew's Day Massacre of 1572 in Paris, when Queen Catherine de' Medici allowed Roman Catholics to murder 3,000 Protestants, Gentillet, a French noble, wrote:

> **20** Queen Catherine was the devil's chosen instrument for spreading the poison of Machiavelli in France.
>
> Quoted by F. Gilbert, *Machiavelli and Guicciardini*, 1965

What extracts from Machiavelli might Gentillet and the leaders of the Roman Catholic Church have used to show that he should be banned?

4 What extracts from pages 74–76 might the writer of source 19 use to show Machiavelli was a 'patriot' [caring for his country] with an 'acute [sharp] understanding of politics'?

5 What do you think are the main changes which have occurred since the sixteenth century which cause Machiavelli to have a far better reputation now than then?

6 The way the term 'machiavellian' is now used in modern English reflects the sixteenth-century opinion of Machiavelli more than the modern one. Why do you think this is so?

6 The Renaissance in Europe

1 Duke Humphrey's Library in Oxford.

1 a) What sort of books did Duke Humphrey (source 1) collect?
b) Why did he ask an Italian to help him with his collection?
2 a) What did Castiglione write about? Where did he get his ideas from?
b) What evidence is there that his book was popular?

Humanism

Humanist ideas quickly caught the imagination of other Europeans. In England, for example, Humphrey, Duke of Gloucester (younger brother of King Henry V), was so impressed by the translations of the Greek philosophers which Florentine humanists had done for him that he asked one of them, Pier Decembrio, to help him improve his collection of classical books. Much of this collection he gave to Oxford University between 1435 and 1444. The building put up to house them, Duke Humphrey's Library, is still in use.

Printing helped the ideas and fashions of the Italian Renaissance to spread. For example, one of the books most read by fashionable European noblemen of the sixteenth century was the *Book of the Courtier* by Baldassare Castiglione. This book, whose author had served at the court of the Duke of Mantua between 1500 and 1524, described how noblemen and women should behave at the courts of kings and princes. It was written in 1516 and published by Aldus Manutius in Venice in 1528. So popular did it become in England that Sir Thomas Hoby translated it into English in 1561.

The new learning in England

There was a two-way traffic in humanist ideas. Italian humanists visited other countries and foreigners travelled to Italy so as to experience humanism directly. From England, William Grocyn, Thomas Linacre and John Colet all studied in Italy in the 1480s and 1490s. Grocyn and Colet both returned to Oxford University, Grocyn to teach Greek and Colet to lecture on the Bible. Linacre, as well as becoming the doctor of King Henry VIII, was appointed tutor to his son, Prince Arthur. He also wrote a Latin textbook for use in schools. Grocyn, Linacre and Colet became leaders of the new humanist learning in England.

The great Dutch humanist and church reformer, Erasmus, who was in England in 1499, was much impressed with what he found. He wrote to an English friend who was studying in Italy:

> **2** It is marvellous how widespread and abundant is the harvest of Ancient learning which is flourishing in this country. All the more reason for your returning to it quickly.
>
> Erasmus, Letter to Robert Fisher, December 1499

Colet, who became Dean of St Paul's Cathedral in 1505, founded a school for 153 pupils in 1512. Pupils there studied Latin and Greek as well as religious instruction. Foreign pupils were welcome and poor pupils paid their way by keeping the school clean.

The humanist school curriculum, based on Latin, Greek and ancient History, became the main diet of European schoolchildren for the next three centuries.

Humanism and church reform

Humanism made educated people critical of the present and of the recent past. Humanists like Colet and Erasmus were convinced Christians but they had a low opinion of the way in which Christian ideas had been taught in the Middle Ages and were still being taught in their own time. They also disliked the manner in which the popes governed the Church from their court in Rome. For example, they objected when the popes sold 'indulgences'. By buying indulgences people bought forgiveness for their sins or for the sins of loved ones. Erasmus wrote to Colet early in 1518:

> **3** The court of Rome clearly has lost all sense of shame; for what could be more shameless than these continued indulgences? Now a war against the Turks is put forth as the reason for raising money, when the real purpose [of the Pope] is to drive the Spaniards from Naples . . . for the Pope's nephew lays claim to Naples. If these troubles continue, the rule of the Turks would be easier to bear than the rule of these Christians.
>
> Erasmus, Letter to John Colet, 1518

The sale of indulgences also led Martin Luther, a professor at the University of Wittenberg in Germany, to protest against what he saw to be an evil custom of the Church. In 1517, Pope Leo X's agents toured Germany, selling indulgences to pay for the rebuilding of St Peter's in Rome. Luther

3 When Erasmus talked about 'the ancient learning' flourishing in England (source 2), what did he mean?

4 For what reasons were Colet and Erasmus (source 3) critical of the Church?

nailed his '95 Theses', which criticised how the popes led the Church, to the door of Wittenberg castle church.

Luther's action marks the beginning of the Reformation which caused a bitter and violent split in the Christian Church between Roman Catholics who stayed loyal to the popes and Protestants who, following Luther's teaching, broke away and formed their own separate churches.

Unlike Luther, Erasmus stayed a member of the Catholic Church. He believed that the Church was better reformed from the inside rather than by splitting away from it.

1 What did Francis Bacon (source 4) like about Machiavelli's writings?

Politics and science

Because they were ready to ask difficult questions about past and present ways of thinking, the Italian humanists paved the way for important advances in politics and science. Francis Bacon, politician and philosopher in early seventeenth-century England, wrote of Machiavelli's political writings:

> **4** We are much beholden [owe a great deal] to Machiavel [Machiavelli] and others, that write what men do and not what they ought to do.
>
> Francis Bacon, *The Advancement of Learning*, 1605

In much the same way as some writers tried to explain what people in power did and why they did it, others were to try to make sense of the natural world. The scientific revolution of the seventeenth century took place because people had become more curious about the world around them. They looked for explanations for things like the movement of the planets or the circulation of the blood, which could be tested against observed facts.

Artistic ideas

The new styles introduced by the artists of the Italian Renaissance completely changed European art. For the next four centuries, few European artists thought their artistic education was finished until they had toured Italy.

Germany

Albrecht Durer (1471–1528) is a good example of Italian influence in Germany. He was a painter and engraver from Nuremberg who spent many years in northern Italy. The painter he most admired was Giovanni Bellini, by then near the end of his life, whose workshops he visited in Venice. His style clearly changed as a result of his interest in Italian art.

5 Durer, St Jerome.

2 Which Italian painter most influenced Durer? How can you tell a Renaissance picture from a Gothic one?

France

In his *Book of the Courtier*, Castiglione suggested that the French were an uncivilised people. He wrote:

6 The French recognise only the nobility of arms, and reckon all the rest as nought; and they consider all educated men to be very base [worthless].

Castiglione, *Book of the Courtier*, published 1528

However, he had great hopes of the future Francis I. Once he became king, Castiglione thought that:

> 7 ... just as the glory of arms flourishes and shines in France, so must civilisation flourish there with the greatest splendour.

Castiglione, *Book of the Courtier*, published 1528

This is very much what happened. The French invasions of Italy caused many Italian artists to work in France. We have seen how Leonardo da Vinci spent his final years in France at the invitation of Francis I (see page 58). Later, in the 1520s and 1530s, Francis made his court at the Palace of Fontainebleau outside Paris into a 'new Rome'. He invited many Italian artists to the palace which he had extended and redecorated in the Renaissance style. Another palace which he had built was Chambord in the Loire valley.

8 Raphael's portrait of Castiglione, done in about 1515.

1 Why was Castiglione (source 6) critical of the French? Of what changes made by Francis I would he have approved?

9 The Palace of Chambord. The building of the palace was begun in 1519 and the architect was an Italian, Domenico da Cortona.

England

English architecture provides a good example of how Italian Renaissance styles spread to other countries. Compare the two buildings shown in sources 10 and 11.

The first (source 10) is by Andrea Palladio (1508–80) who designed many fine buildings in north-east Italy, in and around Venice. He studied the buildings and writings of the architects of ancient Rome and wrote his own *Four Books on Architecture*.

The second (source 11) is by Inigo Jones (1573–1652) who was the chief architect of King Charles I of England. Jones visited Italy twice. He saw most of Palladio's works, along with many others, and read his books on architecture. Between 1616 and 1640, he designed a number of important buildings in the Renaissance style which, for the next two centuries, became the style preferred the English royal family and upper classes (see source 14).

10 Andrea Palladio: Villa Rotonda, designed in 1550.

2 What evidence is there that Inigo Jones was influenced by Italian Renaissance architecture?

3 Unjumble the following words by taking one from each of (i), (ii), and (iii):
(i) Durer; Francis; Palladio; Jones. (ii) architect; architect/writer; king; engraver. (iii) Italian; English; German; French.

11 Inigo Jones: The Queen's House, Greenwich, designed in 1616.

Music

You may have noticed that hardly anywhere in this book has music been mentioned. This may have puzzled you since in Renaissance times as much as today, music was very popular. The reason it has not been mentioned is because it developed quite differently from the other arts, and Italy was not the leader in musical change during the fifteeenth and early sixteenth centuries.

No music survived from ancient times, so musical composers did not use classical Roman and Greek models to break with medieval approaches. There were changes, but they were slower and were made less sharply. Much fifteenth-century music was written for church services, but more and more was composed for the pleasure of kings and nobles, and for dances and other entertainments on public holidays.

The leading composers came from northern Europe. Probably the greatest of the period was Josquin Despres (1440–1521) who was born in Flanders. The Sforza family employed him in Milan and he was at their court at the same time as Leonardo da Vinci, himself an excellent singer and player of the lyre.

No-one doubted Josquin's skill as a composer, but he was not an easy person to work with. In 1500 the Duke of Ferrara needed a new court musician. His agent suggested that there were two strong candidates, Josquin Despres and Heinrich Isaak. Isaak was also from Flanders, but he had been working recently in Florence and had set some of Lorenzo de' Medici's poems to music. The agent reported:

12 It is true that Josquin composes better, but he does it when he feels like it, not when he is asked; and he is demanding 200 ducats while Isaak will be satisfied with 120.

The Duke chose Isaak.

Only later in the sixteenth century, when the other arts were in decline, did Italy take the lead in European music. Andrea Gabrieli (c.1520–1585) and his nephew Giovanni Gabrieli (1557–1612) in Venice, and Palestrina (c.1525–1594) in Rome were and are highly regarded.

A B C D

14 St Paul's Cathedral designed by Sir Christopher Wren (1675–1711).

13 A 1991 model showing how Paternoster Square will look when it is rebuilt.

The lasting influence of Renaissance styles

The lasting popularity of the Renaissance Classical style is shown by source 13, a 1991 plan for the rebuilding of Paternoster Square in the City of London. Though St Paul's Cathedral (source 14) miraculously escaped destruction from the bombing raids of World War II, the area around it was badly damaged and was rebuilt in the 1960s. The fashionable architectural style of the sixties was both simple and severe – flat roofs, straight lines, and plenty of glass and concrete. Architects were against decoration since they believed that buildings should show rather than hide their function. A railway station, for example, should look like a railway station, not like a medieval castle.

Fashions change and in the 1980s many people, with Prince Charles among them, strongly criticised this 1960s 'brutal' style. In its place came more varied, more decorated buildings which copied past styles. The plan for the redevelopment of Paternoster Square is mainly in a 'neo-classical' style, so-called because it used ideas from classical and Renaissance times.

1 What parts of St Paul's Cathedral tell you that it is a Renaissance style building? To which Italian building is it most similar?

2 Look carefully at buildings A and B in source 13. What have they in common with the Renaissance buildings which you have studied?

3 Building C is modelled on a particular Italian building. Which one? (The picture on page 4 will help you.)

4 A born-again Cosimo de' Medici might feel quite at home in the new Paternoster Square. Why? (see pages 10 and 11.)

Review and Assessment

Why was the Italian Renaissance an important period in the history of Europe?

1 Marsilio Ficino, a Florentine humanist, wrote to a German friend, Paul of Middelburg, in 1492:

> **15** If we are to call an age golden, it must certainly be our age which has produced so many golden people. Evidence is provided by the inventions of this age. For this century has restored to light: grammar, poetry, oratory [speech-making], painting, sculpture, architecture, music . . . and all this in Florence.
>
> M. Ficino, Letter to Paul of Middelburg, included in his collected works which were first published in 1576

a List six Florentine artists of the fifteenth century and note whether they were painters, sculptors, or architects.

b Why was the fifteenth century a golden age in Florence?

c How much longer did this golden age last after 1492?

2 Baldassare Castiglione wrote in his *Book of the Courtier* in 1516:

> **16** I would have our Courtier well-educated in letters, at least in those studies which we call the humanities. Let him know not only Latin, but Greek too, because so many and varied matters are written about in those languages.
>
> Castiglione, *Book of the Courtier*, published 1528

a What languages does Castiglione want his Courtier to learn?

b Why does he recommed these languages rather than French or English for example?

c Explain the meaning of the word 'Renaissance'.

3 **a** How can you tell that source 17 is a Renaissance picture?

b Explain why it is a good example of the use of perspective.

c How well, in your opinion, does it compare with modern city plans?

17 Piero della Francesca drew this picture of an *Ideal Town* in about 1460.

4 Francesco Guicciardini wrote in his *Ricordi* [Reflections]:

18 It is impossible to control governments, if you want to control them nowadays, according to Christian rules . . . All political power is rooted in violence . . . I include priests in this rule – indeed their power is double since they use both worldly and religious weapons to control us.

F. Guicciardini, *Ricordi* [Reflections], 1528–30

a What had Guicciardini lived through which made him so certain that political power was rooted in violence?

b Give examples of both the worldly and religious weapons which the popes could use against their enemies.

c Name another political writer whose views were similar to those of Guicciardini. In what ways did such political views mark a break with the past?

5 **a** What first do you look for to tell the 'Gothic' style in the arts from the 'Renaissance' style?

b Describe the most important changes, giving examples where possible, which the Italian Renaissance brought to (i) architecture, (ii) sculpture, and (iii) painting. How far did these changes spread outside Italy?

6 What was humanism? Describe its effects across Europe on **a** education, **b** religion and **c** science.

INDEX